R.G. Pedley   Gawsworth   April 1976.

MR SMITH'S
FLOWER GARDEN

by Geoffrey Smith

Illustrated by Colin Gray

Edited by Brian Davies

BRITISH BROADCASTING CORPORATION

Published to accompany the BBC-tv series Mr Smith's Flower Garden produced by Peter Riding and Brian Davies and first broadcast on BBC-2 on Fridays at 7.05 p.m. from 21st May – 18th June 1976.

Published to accompany a series of programmes prepared in consultation with the BBC Further Education Advisory Council.

Other BBC books by the author
Mr Smith's Gardening Book
Mr Smith's Vegetable Garden

The photographs on front and back covers and page 3 were specially taken by Arthur Smith of Rose Productions.

©Geoffrey Smith and the British Broadcasting Corporation 1976
First published 1976
Published by the British Broadcasting Corporation, 35 Marylebone High Street, London, W1M 4AA.
Set in 9/10pt Plantin 110 Monophoto
Printed in England by Alan Pooley Limited,
Tunbridge Wells, Kent.
ISBN: 0 563 16013 6

Introduction

I doubt whether all the books on gardening combined into one volume, if this were possible, could supply answers to all the questions a garden poses. This book will, I hope, encourage even the beginner in gardening to obtain good results.

No two gardens are alike, and this book is about a garden I worked in during one year. That there was a television camera filming the bedding-out, pruning, or cutting-taking made no difference to my gardening. Habits are so ingrained and the work captures my interest so completely, that a film crew is just another less common garden pest to contend with.

The cultivation of ornamental plants allows the gardener an outlet for the creative, artistic expressions which is an inherent part of all human beings.

Design a garden to suit your own personal taste, no matter if no one else likes it, providing you as a gardener are content, that is enough. Fortunately, as yet, no government legislation has been passed to insist that we all grow the same plants. In gardening we please ourselves. The choice of designs and plants to fit them is almost limitless. I hope this book will at least be a guide to some of the avenues of exploration.

Geoffrey Smith

CONTENTS

Roses 4
Bedding Plants 16
Patio and Tub Plants 24
House and Pot Plants 29
The Mixed Border 38
Monthly calendar of work 46

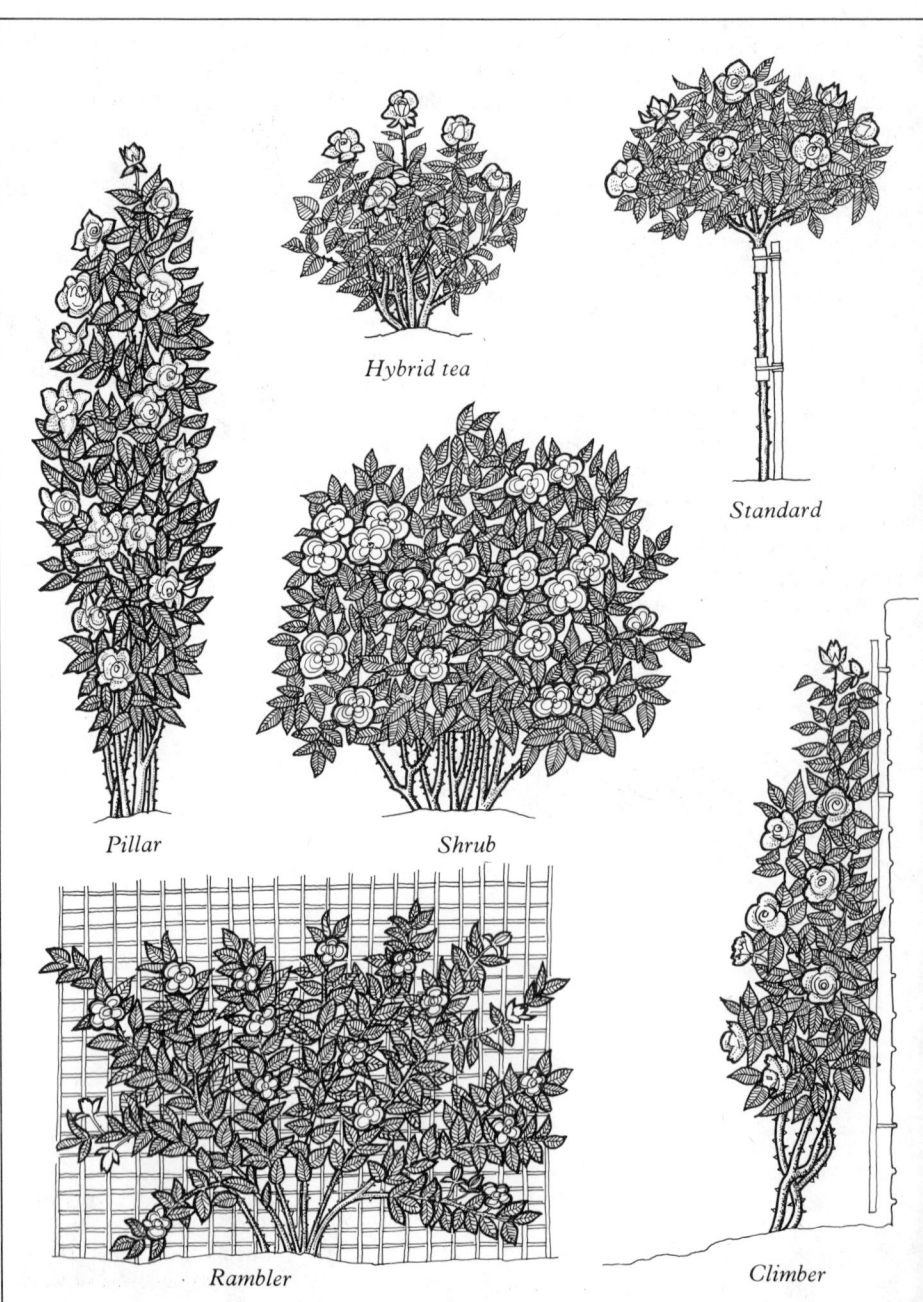

1 Roses

For centuries the rose has been cultivated as a garden shrub, so it is not surprising that through selective breeding an enormous number of varieties have been produced. Indeed, it would be true to say there is a rose to fill every need from the 6-inch high miniature, suitable for window box cultivation, to the vigorous climbers which in three years will cover 200 square feet of wall.

Making a choice from a nursery list where each plant is described in glowing terms is not easy. Roses will grow in most soils and situations, although more effort is required to maintain healthy bushes on sand or chalk land than on a free draining loam. An open position will be more acceptable than a site shaded by a building or tall trees.

Hybrid tea

The modern bedding roses flower from JUNE to OCTOBER, and by following a few basic rules anyone can grow first class blooms. Bearing all these points in mind, the would be rose grower need only worry about height and colour which makes the choice considerably easier.

In between there are climbers, ramblers, standards, pillar and shrub roses, all with a contribution to make somewhere in the garden. The bedding roses, hybrid tea and floribunda, are the most frequently grown. Hybrid tea have generally double flowers on long stems, useful for garden display or as cut blooms. Floribunda may be double, single, or any of the permutations between. Usually the flowers are carried in a large terminal clustered head which makes them excellent value for massed planting in formal beds. They can also be grown in the shrub or herbaceous border but are then only lightly pruned.

Floribunda

Choose the most open situation the garden offers for the rose bed. Sunlight and free air circulation are better than all the chemical sprays ever invented for maintaining healthy roses.

SOIL

All roses have one basic requirement – the soil they are to be grown in must be well prepared, for though roses will survive in poor soil, they flower less freely and become prone to disease.

Prepare the soil at least four weeks in advance of planting. I prefer to double dig (1) and manure the bed in Autumn, then plant the following MARCH, but bedding roses can be planted at any time from OCTOBER to MARCH, during the dormant period. Chalk soils will benefit from dressings of acid peat. On badly drained soils, raise the bed 6 inches or more above that of the general level. Surplus water drains

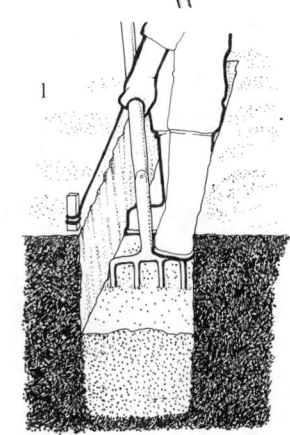

away and the risk of stagnant water causing root rot is very much reduced.

A month after digging check to see if the soil needs lime. Though roses will grow in both alkaline and acid land they show a marked preference for a soil just on the acid side of neutral. Lime is an essential plant food, but the texture of some soils, particularly acid clay, is very much improved by a dressing of lime. A simple test with one of the chemicals obtainable at most horticultural sundriesmen shops determines the nature of a soil. The acidity or alkalinity is expressed in the form of a table; pH7 is neutral, any reading below means the soil is acid, any above shows there is lime present. Continuous annual dressings of fertilizer and compost or manure will tend to make soil acid, so further tests should be done at yearly intervals.

When a rose needs replacing DO NOT replant into the same soil – either move the position of the bed to a site which has not grown roses for five years, or change the soil to a depth of 14 inches. Continual replanting of roses into the soil can lead to a condition known as soil sickness where the bushes sicken and die. There is no cure except a change of soil.

The soil in a rose bed tends to shrink, leaving the crowns exposed. Prevent this by spreading a layer of compost, peat, or well rotted manure on top of the soil each year after pruning. This is known as mulching. Roses are expensive but with care will last 10–15 years. Once planted little can be done to improve the soil, apart from feeding and mulching, so work in all the manure, compost or similar organic matter available when the bed is being prepared. Before Winter the bush roses should be lightly pruned to prevent the gales loosening the roots in the soil.

PLANTING

Choose and order the roses well in advance of planting time as orders are booked then dispatched by the nurseries on the first come first served principle. Late comers find either the varieties chosen are sold out or, even worse, only second class plants are left.

A good rose bush will have a strong fibrous root system with at least three vigorous shoots springing from it (1). Buying from a local rose grower is often worthwhile as it is possible to collect the order when it is required. Any defect in quality can be noted and rectified by the nurseryman immediately.

The bushes are planted directly they arrive if the bed is ready to receive them. Should the soil be frozen or wet then

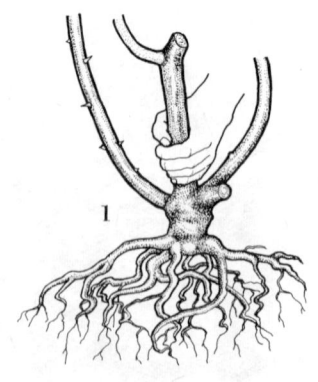

dig out a trench on a sheltered border, lay the roots in this and cover them with soil. This is a garden practice known as heeling-in (1).

For two or three days the plants will be quite safe left as packed from the nursery in a cool airy shed. After that time they should be either heeled-in or planted. Planting can take place at any time from OCTOBER to MARCH. Bushes grown in containers can be moved in any month of the year as the roots suffer no major disturbance. They do cost a little more.

When the soil is in good crumbly condition planting is simple and straightforward. Take out a hole large enough and wide enough to accommodate the roots comfortably when spread out. The depth should be adjusted so the crown (point where branch and roots join) is buried approximately 1 inch deep. Lightly tip all the roots (2), cutting those which are bruised or broken back to sound wood. This stimulates the rapid development of new fibrous roots which soon take hold in their new position. Space out the roots evenly across the base of the hole (3) working the soil between them and firming until the required level is achieved. Leave the soil surface loose so the rain can penetrate easily. Remember rose roots are active long before there is any sign of leaves, so do not delay planting beyond early MARCH. When soil conditions are wet make up a mixture of two parts soil, two parts peat and one part sand to work round the roots at planting time.

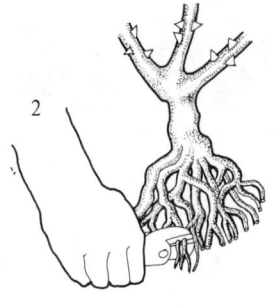

Hybrid tea and floribunda roses planted in late FEBRUARY to MARCH may be pruned before insertion, cutting all shoots back to within two or three buds of the base. As a result of hard pruning, young strong shoots break from low down to build up a strong framework for flower production. Shoots growing in the wrong direction should be rubbed out with the fingers before they harden. A few moments spent on this early training will make certain of a well shaped bush, and is a leisurely way to occupy a warm Spring evening.

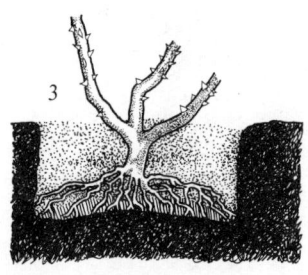

The same care should be exercised in planting standard roses and in addition they must be firmly staked. Standard roses are usually grown on stems of the wild dog rose *(Rosa canina)* or the species *R. rugosa*. The two are fairly easily identified – *canina* has almost smooth stems whereas *rugosa* is a mass of prickles. Buds of the required variety are inserted in the stems *(rugosa)* or side branches *(canina)* at about 4–5 feet above soil level. Shoots which break from these buds are trained to form a framework of branches known as a head. When carrying a full load of leaves and flowers the head may be broken off in strong winds which is

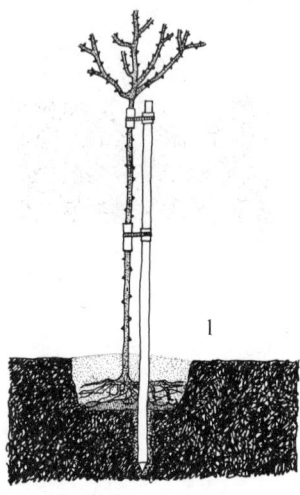

why staking is necessary. Dig a hole, set the stake firmly in place, position the tree, replace the soil as with bush roses. Two ties will be necessary – one just below the head, another half way up the stem (1). If the stem is liable to rub on the ·stake, protect the area with sacking or similar material. Standards usually arrive ready pruned so only cut out damaged shoots.

Climbing or rambling roses are expensive so give them a good start especially if they are grown on a house wall. Soil at the base of a wall tends to be poor and dry. Remove the existing soil then replace it at planting time with a compost made up of 5 loam, 2 peat and a 5-inch potfull of bone meal or fish meal to every barrow load of mixture. Bend the stem out so instead of the roots running directly down the base of the wall they are stepped out 6–9 inches out of the dry area (2). Keep well watered in dry season and make sure the planting is below the level of the damp course. Tie the stems to a support after planting.

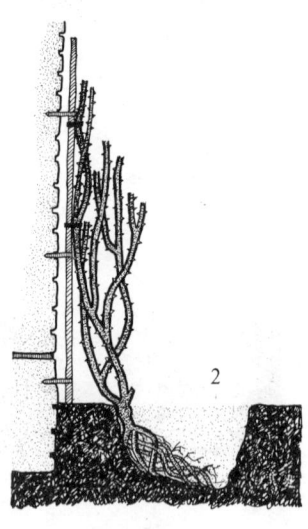

With newly planted ramblers all shoots are cut back to a healthy bud, strong shoots to 18 inches, weak shoots back to the base. The growth which break from these are trained on to supports fixed to a wall with bobbins. The bobbins are made by cutting a piece of hard wood into 2 inch long sections. Trellis nailed to these stands clear of the wall allowing air to circulate which reduces the incidence of disease. DO NOT grow other plants closer than 20 inches from base of rose.

Weeds must be kept under control as they complete with the roses for water and food. A push hoe used at regular intervals solves the weed problem – DO NOT use a spade or fork as these damage the roots and may cause 'suckering'. Suckers are strong shoots which grow from below soil level. These have to be removed by pulling them away from as near to the point where they emerge from the root as possible. DO NOT cut them away because this just encourages more growth.

FEEDING

All roses need feeding – 2 oz balanced fertilizer to the square yard in Spring after pruning plus a mulch of rotted manure, compost or peat in MAY to keep the roots moist. In early JULY a further 2 oz of fertiliser will help the bushes to keep on producing flowers.

A balanced fertiliser contains:
NITROGEN – essential for strong growth and healthy foliage. Deficiency causes yellowing of leaves.

PHOSPHATES to build up a strong root system. Deficiency indicated by purplish tints on the underside of very green leaves.

POTASH for flower colour and disease resistance. Deficiency causes brittle edges of leaves.

Trace elements should not be in short supply on a soil supplied with compost or rotted manure. Magnesium is the most common deficiency, corrected by a teaspoonful of Epsom Salts to a gallon of water sprayed over the foliage once a month from APRIL to AUGUST.

Foliar feeding (spraying nutriment in solution over the leaves) is an expensive way to feed roses – most of the liquid runs off to the roots in any case. I only use it if growth is slow on newly planted roses because of a cold soil in Spring.

Roses need a constant supply of moisture. Mulching (1) will help but during periods of very dry weather watering will be necessary. Give the soil a thorough soaking – damping over the top inch of soil is useless. Mulching helps to keep the soil moist in the Summer, adds humus to the soil, and reduces the risk of infection by covering up spores of fungus diseases, e.g. *blackspot*. Some suitable materials are peat, well rotted manure or compact leaf mould or grass clippings. Make sure that the grass is relatively weed free and hasn't been treated with weed killer before using grass cuttings. Mulching should be done in MAY to JUNE.

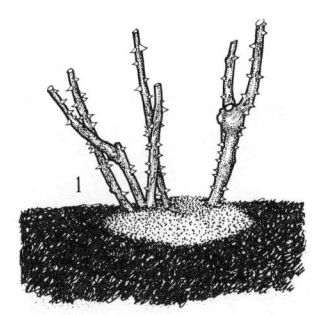

1

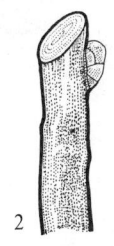

2

Right

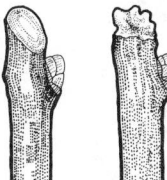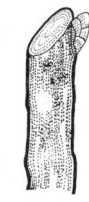

Wrong

PRUNING

Almost all roses need some pruning to keep them in good healthy growth and flowering well.

Unpruned they produce a mass of twiggy, tangled growth, dead wood and small flowers. They are also shorter lived.

When pruning use a sharp pair of secateurs so the cuts made are clean with no torn or ragged edges (2). Cut in the same direction as an outward facing bud – a sloping wound close enough to the bud so there is no fear of *die back*, but not so close that the bud is killed, about ¼ inch is ideal.

Hybrid Tea Cut away all dead, damaged or weak shoots. The remainder are pruned back to six buds on strong shoots, three buds on the less vigorous (3). Hard pruning tends to encourage stronger growth which is the reason why weak shoots need to be cut back severely. When H.T. or floribunda roses are grown as shrubs, pruning is less severe – back to eight or ten buds on strong wood and six on the weak.

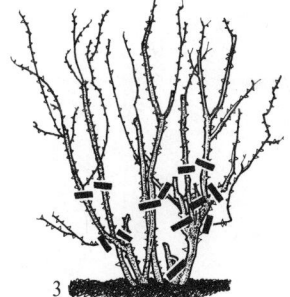

3

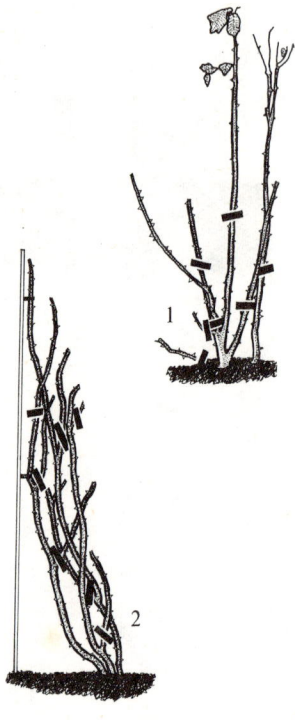

Floribunda, and this includes varieties classified as Polyantha roses, tend to be stronger growing than the H.T. so they are not cut back quite so hard. First remove dead, damaged or weak wood then prune the strong growths back to seven or eight buds from the base, weak shoots to two or three buds (1). Floribunda roses very lightly pruned soon run to thin twiggy growths and severe pruning makes for too vigorous shoots which flower a fortnight later than bushes correctly treated.

Standard H.T. roses are pruned just like an H.T. bush – the purpose being to build up a strong, well spaced framework of flowering shoots.

Standard floribunda are pruned like the bush floribunda.

Climbing roses are dealt with in late FEBRUARY to MARCH. Leave the framework of branches spaced out on the trellis untouched providing they are healthy. Cut back the short growths on the framework branches to two or three buds (2). The flowers mature on these shoots in JUNE. Strong young shoots may be left to replace the old framework branches when necessary.

Everblooming climbers need little attention apart from removal of dead heads, worn out and weak growths.

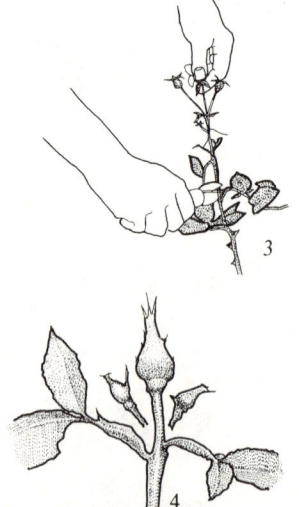

Rambling roses usually have one crop of flowers in JUNE to JULY so may be pruned immediately the display is finished. Cut the old stems which have flowered right out at ground level. As the young growths develop they are tied in to replace them and will flower the following Summer.

Weeping standards Cut away all the stems which have carried blooms to make way for the young growths. These are tied to the wire framework to form a neat symmetrical head.

Bedding roses – both H.T. and floribunda will need the dead flowers removing at regular intervals during the blossoming period (3). Spent flower stems are cut back to the first bud (leaf joint). To get show quality H.T. blooms some removal of surplus buds will be required (4). Leave the top larger bud and remove the small buds which grow out immediately below it so all the available food is directed to the one which is retained.

Roses for display are cut either in late evening or early morning. Take the longest stalk possible, choose those where the flowers are about half open. The cut should not be more than one third of the flowering stem, and should be made directly above an outward facing bud. Before arranging, plunge for several hours up to the base of the flower in a bucket of cold water. This deep soaking is important if the roses are to be entered in competition at the local show. The stems become fully charged with moisture and will then remain fresh for much longer, even in a warm room or tent.

PROPAGATION

Roses are usually propagated by taking a bud from the required variety and inserting it into a suitable root stock. Late JUNE, JULY and AUGUST are the most suitable months for this work. They will also root from cuttings taken at any time between late JULY and mid-NOVEMBER. Shoots removed during dead-heading will root. Cut with a sharp knife below a leaf joint and remove the lower leaves (1). Dip the cut surface in rooting powder then insert the cutting in sharp sand (2) made up in a frame for preference, or direct into the open garden. Where only one or two extra bushes are required, push the cuttings into a 6-inch flower pot filled with a mixture of two parts sharp sand, and one part peat. They should be watered well and then placed inside a polythene bag which is fastened around the pot sides with a rubber band. This keeps the moisture in and the cuttings root so much quicker.

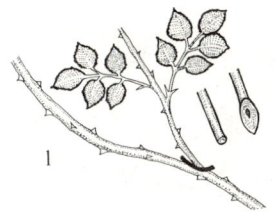

Ramblers may be propagated by pulling down a young stem, making a slit on the underside then pegging it down into a compost of two parts sand, one part peat. Roots develop from the cut surface and when these are large enough, the branch is cut from the parent and lifted the following Spring.

PESTS AND DISEASES

Roses do suffer from pests and diseases but the risk of attack may be reduced by buying good plants from a reputable grower. Never leave dead wood and leaves lying about, burn them; prepare the ground well before planting – a lot of rose troubles are caused by poor drainage; DO NOT plant bushes too close together; feed plants properly. Good cultivations lessen the risk of an attack but even in the best run gardens some spraying may be necessary.

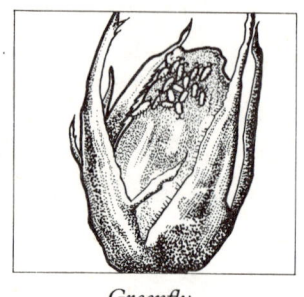
Greenfly

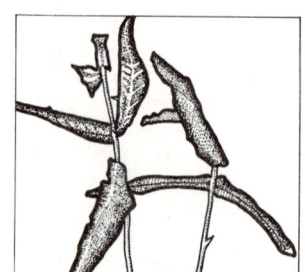
Sawfly caterpillar

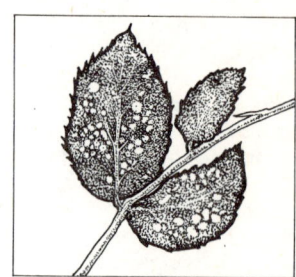
Leafhopper

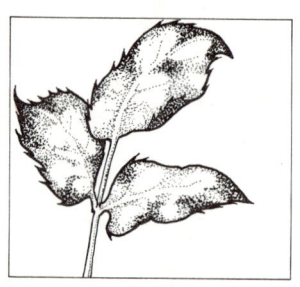
Powdery mildew

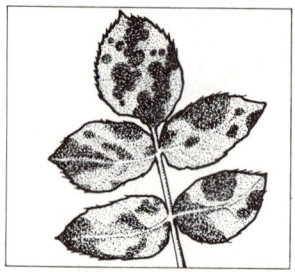
Black spot

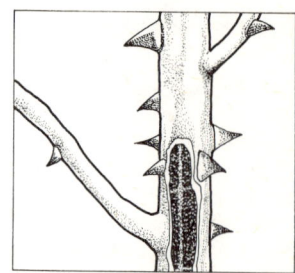
Canker

Capsid bug

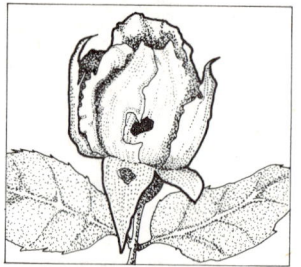
Tortrix moth caterpillar

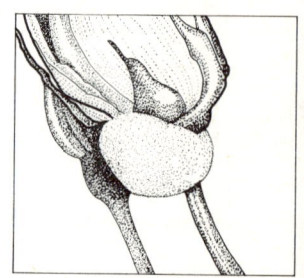
Froghopper

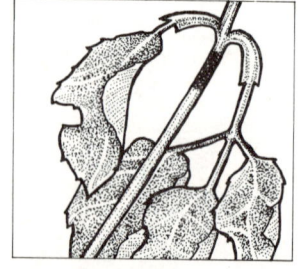
Dieback

Thrips

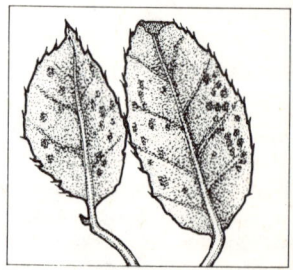
Rust

Greenfly infest shoot tips and flower buds. They are the most common and serious of all pests. They cause distorted growth and can prevent buds from opening.

Sawfly caterpillars feed on the developing leaves. They can roll the leaves up to form a tent for protection.

Leafhoppers – small yellowish insects, feed on the leaves sucking the sap and causing a freckling of the leaf – pale yellow patches.

All can be controlled by spraying with a systemic insecticide (one taken up into the sap stream of the plant) or derris pyrethrum. In fact, there are a dozen proprietary sprays available which will do the work.

Powdery mildew forms a white coating on young leaves, flower buds and stems. It can cause leaf cockling and leaves fall early as a result. It usually takes place in Summer or early Autumn and is frequently found in closed-in positions, e.g. near a wall and during hot weather in daytime and cold at night.

Black spot causes dark brown spots on the foliage and is commonly found in moist areas – thought to be due to warm, wet conditions and a shortage of potash. It is very rarely found in industrial parts. Spray at fourteen day intervals from JUNE onwards with a proprietary spray. Gather up the prunings and fallen leaves, then burn them to kill overwintering spores. DO NOT plant the bushes too deeply.

Canker – wounds on stems which split open to expose underlying tissue usually surrounded by corky material – they should be cut away to clean wood.

Capsid bug feeds on the tips of young shoots – a systemic spray will give a control.

Tortrix moth caterpillars – these feed on the flower and the foliage. Control by hand picking or a systemic insecticide.

Froghopper – identified by frothy spittle in which it hides – systemic spray or malathion through a coarse spray will control.

Dieback – starts in dead wood (spurs left by poor pruning). Cut back to healthy growth.

Thrips feed on developing buds, especially bad in hot dry weather – spray with malathion.

Rust – bright orange patches on the leaves. It may be encouraged by water shortage. Keep the beds watered and mulched. Spray with colloidal copper during the Winter. In Summer spray with Bordeaux mixture or one of the proprietary chemicals at monthly intervals.

Red spider Spray with systemic insecticide at regular intervals during the Summer or petroleum white oil. During the Winter, when bushes are completely dormant, spray with tar oil Winter wash.

Mineral deficiencies do occur on some soils. Regular applications of fertiliser and mulches of organic matter should prove an adequate safeguard.

Six choice hybrid tea roses

'E. H. MORSE' Well formed red blooms, fragrant and useful for cutting. Height 30 inches.

'GRANDPA DICKSON' Upright growth, creamy yellow flowers. Height 3 feet.

'PEACE' Vigorous growth, dark green foliage, flowers pale yellow edged with pink. Prune lightly. Height up to 6 feet.

'STELLA' Strong disease resistant growth, flowers pale pink with a deeper edge. Height 3 feet.

'SUTTERS GOLD' Tall upright growth, flowers orange with slight fragrance. Height 3 feet.

'WENDY CUSSONS' Vigorous growth, flowers cerise deepening to scarlet – very fragrant. Height 3 feet 6 inches.

Six choice floribunda roses

'ALLGOLD' Deep golden yellow, flowers freely. Height 24–30 inches.

'BLESSINGS' Vigorous growth, flowers fragrant coral pink. Height 3 feet.

'EVELYN FISON' Disease resistant foliage, scented vivid red flowers. Height 30 inches.

'MARLENE' Low growing, compact scarlet flowers freely produced. Height 15 inches.

'MOONRAKER' Creamy white flowers carried in abundance from JUNE well into Autumn. Height 30 inches.

'ORANGE SENSATION' Upright vigorous growth, weather resistant orange flowers. Height 30 inches – 3 feet.

Miniature roses

'CORALIN' Coral pink flushed orange, semi-double flowers. Height 12 inches.

'PEON' Deep crimson with a white eye. Height 8 inches.

'PIXIE' Apple blossom pink double flowers. Height 9 inches.

'ROSINA' Well formed, full double, clear yellow flowers. Height 12 inches.

Climbers

'CAROLINE TESTOUT' Will grow up to 10 feet high with pink flowers which are strongly scented.

'MAIGOLD' Best grown as a wall shrub for the branches are thickly covered in thorns. The bronze on yellow blooms are scented. Height 12 feet.

'SCHOOLGIRL' A strong disease resistant rose, the apricot flowers are sweetly scented. Height 10 feet.

Ramblers

'ALBERTINE' A well tried favourite with copper pink flowers delightfully scented. May be subject to mildew on some soils. Height 16 feet.

'CRIMSON SHOWER' A vigorous hybrid growing up to 8 feet. Small crimson flowers carried in trusses in JULY to AUGUST.

'EASLEA'S GOLDEN RAMBLER' A strong growing variety. The double yellow flowers are scented and contrast pleasantly with the dark glossy green foliage. DO NOT prune until well established. Height 10 feet.

Weeping standards

There are few roses which weep naturally. I would consider 'CRIMSON SHOWER' and 'EXCELSA' (double crimson) amongst the best.

Shrub roses

'FRED LOADS' A tall growing floribunda up to 7 feet high. The single bright orange flowers are produced over 2 or 3 months – slightly fragrant.

'FRITZ NOBIS' will make a rounded bush 5 feet high. The semi-double, deep pink flowers borne in JUNE to JULY are clover scented.

'HEIDELBERG' Vigorous disease resistant shrub up to 6 feet high. Large bright red flowers in clustered heads.

'LADY SONIA' Erect growing shrub up to 6 feet. The H.T. type flowers semi-double, deep yellow streaked with dark red.

2 Bedding Plants

Summer flowering annuals are an exciting part of gardening, because they can be grown from seed to flower in a matter of 12 weeks. The owner of a new house, faced with a barren piece of earth, can transform it almost overnight by filling the emptiness with annuals. No special skill is required providing inexperience is balanced with a little common sense.

Each year the cost of a box of annuals increases, so of necessity more people are going to raise their own bedding plants from seed. Essential equipment includes seed trays, either plastic or wood, of a standard size 14½ inches by 8½ inches, 2 or 3 inches deep. Provision is made at the bottom for drainage – wooden trays have space left between the slats, plastic trays have holes drilled in the base. Pots, clay or plastic have a drainage hole in the bottom.

The seeds are sown into trays or pots, then pricked off for growing on. A dozen or so trays should be enough. Use the John Innes compost or one of the peat based mixtures, both seed and potting; a deep bowl to plunge the pots into for watering; some sheets of glass and newspaper to cover the pots after the seed is sown. Air, moisture, warmth and available nutriment are four essentials, then, once the leaves develop, light is needed so growth can continue. A warm frame or windowsill is an ideal place for seedlings to grow.

The half pot is in many ways like the maternity ward of a hospital, everything has to be clean and sterile. Unless the pot is brand new, wash it thoroughly, then put some broken clay pot or a piece of perforated zinc over the drainage holes. A layer of roughage (peat or pea gravel) to make certain all surplus moisture runs away, then the remaining space is topped up to within half an inch of the rim with a suitable compost. Whether it is John Innes, peat based or a home made mixture, it should be free from harmful chemicals, pests, disease and weeds. Firm the surface with the hands (1) or a pot press – any smooth surfaced tin or bottle will do. The levelling is very important with fine seeds like begonia which get washed into the crevices and are then buried too deeply. Always sow seeds thinly. Large seeds like cornflowers may be spaced out individually, small seeds should be mixed with a quantity of fine sand or brick dust to ensure they are evenly distributed. Cover large seeds with their own depth of soil (2), small seeds are just firmed lightly into the compost without covering. Stand the pot up to its rim in a bowl of water (3) to soak the compost thoroughly, cover with glass and a sheet of newspaper to conserve moisture, then place in a warm position.

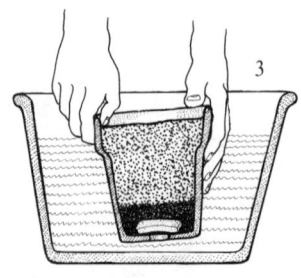

Immediately the seeds are germinated, remove the newspaper to let in the light. Excessive heat can cause weak growth or prevent germination altogether. Avoid temperatures below 40 degrees F or above 75 degrees F; for most plants 55–65 degrees F is ideal. Seedlings are better pricked off into a large container like a seed tray immediately they are large enough to handle, as root disturbance then is minimal. Spacing depends on how long they are to remain in the tray and the ultimate size of the plant, but up to 35 plants to a standard tray is usual. Use an old table fork to lift the seedlings (1) and always handle them by the leaf tips (2) never the stem. Use a blunt pointed stick (dibber) to make the hole, insert the roots and firm GENTLY.

Keep the newly pricked off seedlings close and warm for a few days then gradually harden them off for planting outdoors. The hardening process should be done gradually in a cold frame; ventilate a little more each day (3) until the protection is removed altogether. Plant half-hardy annuals out in late MAY early JUNE when all fear of frost is past.

Some half-hardy annuals are best potted individually before being transplanted to the open ground – a good example of a strong growing annual would be salvia. Others like antirrhinums should have the growing point removed to make the plants develop more flowering shoots.

The best results are obtained by keeping the plants supplied with adequate moisture, nutriment, warmth, and in a good light throughout every stage of their development.

Prepare the soil which is to grow the Summer bedding plants with the same thoroughness as for any other crop. DO NOT use fresh manure as this encourages the plants to produce a mass of soft leafy growth and few flowers.

Dig the soil over, burying the annual weeds at least 10 inches deep. At the same time work in 2 spadefuls of rotted manure, compost or peat to each square yard. This organic dressing is sufficient to keep the soil in a good physical condition without making it over fertile. Three or four days before the plants are to be bedded out dress the soil with one or two ounces per sq. yard of fish meal or similar fertilizer. Whatever the fertilizer used, it should not be high nitrogen which, again, encourages leaf growth. Rake the soil down until there are no hard clods and the surface is level (4). On heavy soil it is advisable to raise the general height of the bed a few inches above that of the surrounding soil. Annuals must have good drainage – a waterlogged soil can cause root rot. After planting, if the weather is at all dry, thoroughly water the soil. Spraying the foliage over in the cool of the evening will be beneficial to bedding plants.

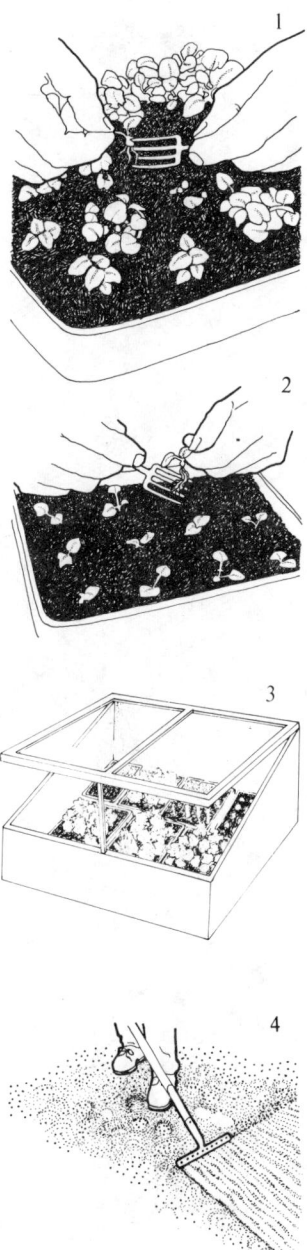

Routine maintenance during the Summer is usually restricted to keeping the bed weed free. As the blooms fade, remove them to prevent seeding and to encourage a further display of blossom.

SPRING DESIGNS

The antirrhinums and other Summer flowering annuals should be removed early enough in the Autumn for the soil to be prepared for polyanthus, viola, wallflowers and bulbs. Remove all perennial weeds, rake in the fertilizer dressing or prick the soil over 3 or 4 inches deep with a fork. Allow six or seven days for the land to 'work' then carry out the planting. Avoid the temptation, especially if the Autumn weather is warm and there is still plenty of flower, to leave the Summer bedding in too long. Spring bedding plants need to be in position while the soil is still warm enough for the roots to establish.

Bellis

Bellis (Double Daisy) a popular perennial plant especially amongst children, the double pom-pom flowers range in colour from white, through pink to deep crimson.

Sow during MAY in a frame or nursery bed. Grow on during the Summer, then transplant to the bed in SEPTEMBER to OCTOBER for flowering in the following Spring. Try the 'Double Carpet' mixture with button flowers in shades of rose red and white on 6 inch stems. A bed of deep yellow tulips edged with daisy 'Double Carpet' makes a lovely picture on a warm Spring day.

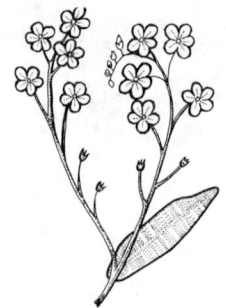
Myosotis

Myosotis (Forget-me-Not). An annual which will combine with every type of Spring bedding including the formal tulip. The misty blue haze of flowers looks equally effective in light shade or full sun. A plant that often seeds itself.

Sow the seeds in a frame or nursery bed during early JUNE in drills (shallow trenches ¼-inch deep). Transplant to positions in SEPTEMBER, ready for flowering the following Spring.

Polyanthus and Primroses are popular perennials. Sow seed in FEBRUARY to MARCH in a frame or greenhouse, harden off for 'growing on' outdoors during Summer. Transfer to the beds in SEPTEMBER for flowering the following Spring. After flowering, lift and divide the choicest colour forms to plant up again the following Winter. Most attractive when combined with Winter flowering viola and 'Forget-me-Not'.

Polyanthus

Viola is a perennial that looks most attractive as a ground cover under tulips or in contrast to the Forget-me-Not.

Sow the seed in late JUNE or JULY into a frame or nursery bed. In very hot weather germination and growth is better if light shade is provided. Transplant to the beds in SEPTEMBER for flowering the following Spring. Because viola like a soil which is cool and moisture retentive, work in a little moist peat before planting up. Select plants are lifted in late MAY and transferred to a nursery bed, then clipped hard. The young shoots which grow are taken as cuttings to grow on for planting in Autumn as Spring bedding.

Spring bulbs Tulips, narcissus, muscari, scilla and crocus are Spring flowering bulbs which combine well with the bedding plants, but where Summer bedding is practised, narcissus, scilla, muscari and crocus are better omitted, as the bulbs do best if left to naturalise without disturbance. However, tulips and hyacinths can be lifted and heeled-in elsewhere to ripen. Take out a shallow trench, lay the bulbs in this and lightly cover with soil, leaving the foliage exposed. The display will not be as good the following year, but bulbs are expensive so the effort is worthwhile.

Viola

SUMMER BEDDING

Half-hardy annuals which are suitable for Summer flowering in both formal beds and to give colour in the shrub or herbaceous border can be bought in many varieties. Some have a brief season of flower, others will only do well in a fine Summer or are prone to disease in certain soils.

There are well tried bedding plants which will, in most years and over a wide range of soils, make a colourful display.

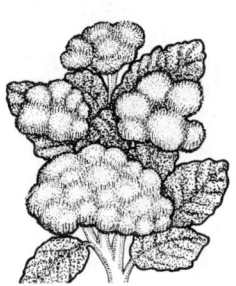

Ageratum

Ageratum An annual, useful as an edging plant or in a mini-border. The variety 'Blue Blazer' 5 inches high with mauve flowers or 'Blue Chip' will carry blooms from JUNE to SEPTEMBER. Place 6 inches apart in late MAY, early JUNE from seed sown in MARCH. Ageratum combines very well with the copper red or yellow marigolds.

Antirrhinum are usually grown as half-hardy annuals and they are one of the most useful of Summer bedding plants. They should be sown in a seed compost of 2 parts rubbed peat, 1 part sand, as excess nitrogen in the standard composts is a major cause of damping off.

Antirrhinum

The seedlings should be pricked off into trays when large enough to handle. Seeds sown in early MARCH are ready for planting in the beds by late MAY, and will flower from JUNE onwards.

The 'Intermediate' varieties which grow 14–18 inches high are free flowering yet neat enough for even formal beds. 'Coronette', 'Floral Cluster' and 'Monarch' can all be obtained true to colour – white, rose, yellow, scarlet, orchid and dark red. Grown with yellow tagetes, the orchid shade is most effective, while the yellow hybrids show best with ageratum or dark blue verbena. The planting distance is 10 inches, so that when fully grown, the bed presents an unbroken carpet of colour.

Aster A half-hardy annual. Difficult to grow on soils which are heavy or badly drained. In spite of this they are attractive enough to be included in a select list. When in doubt grow the 'Wilt Resistant Strain'.

Sow the seeds in a heated frame or greenhouse in MARCH. Prick the seedlings off either into boxes or singly into pots and grow them on, gradually hardening them off for planting out in early JUNE. They will flower later in the same month.

Good varieties – 'Milady Rose' and 'Milady Blue'. Neat compact growth up to 10 inches with large double flowers $2\frac{1}{2}$–3 inches across are carried in succession over several months.

Groups of blue and pink aster interspersed with the silver foliaged *Cineraria maritima* look superbly elegant, both are planted 10 inches apart.

Aster

Begonia The fibrous rooted begonia, a half-hardy annual, can be relied on, irrespective of the prevailing Summer weather, to give continuous colour in the borders from mid-JUNE to OCTOBER.

Seeds are sown in MARCH mixed with sand or brick dust onto the surface of a peat based compost, they are not covered, just lightly firmed. Until germination takes place, water by immersing the pot up to the rim in a dish of water. A minimum temperature of 65 degrees F is essential for even germination. Prick out, harden off and bed out 6 inches apart in the first week in JUNE for flowering by the end of the same month.

Begonia 'F1. Hybrid Compact' varieties grow only 6 inches high, while the equally free flowering 'Indian Maid', 'Organdie' and 'Carmen' reach 9 inches.

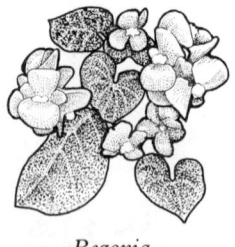

Begonia

As an under planting to pastel flowered standard fuchsia, fibrous rooted begonia have few equals for wealth of blossom and they will also do well in partial shade.

Lobelia A half-hardy annual which is usually grown as an edging to contrast or complement taller, more brightly coloured annuals. For this work choose a self colour, 'Royal', 'Cambridge', or 'Bright Blue', all growing 4 inches high. For planting a small bed, try lobelia 'String of Pearls' a mixture of pink, red, white, blue and purple flowered hybrids.

Sow the seed in early MARCH under glass, DO NOT COVER, just press lightly into the surface of the compost. Prick out into seed trays in groups of 4–6 for growing on. Harden off and plant outdoors in prepared beds, 6 inches apart in JUNE, for flowering later in the month.

Scarlet salvia with an edging of blue lobelia is an eye catching combination.

Lobelia

Marigolds The gayest, most carnival of all bedding, annuals. The seed is sown in a greenhouse during MARCH, pricked out and grown on for planting out in late MAY, ready for flowering in the middle of JUNE.

'Gold Galore' golden yellow, 12–15 inches; 'Spun Gold', 10 inches; 'Red Brocade' mahogany red, 10 inches; 'Harmony' orange and mahogany, 6 inches. Particularly suitable for growing with a contrasting or complementary coloured 'Coronette Antirrhinum'.

Marigold

Pansy The 'Heart's Ease' of cottage gardens is really a perennial bedding plant. Sown in JULY then planted up during OCTOBER, it will carry a succession of flowers from MAY until OCTOBER the following year.

To flower as Summer bedding, sow in a greenhouse or frame during MARCH, prick out into boxes then plant outdoors in late MAY. Pansy and viola should not be grown in the same bed year after year or there may be a build up of the disease known as pansy sickness, which kills the roots. A sprinkling of 4% calomel in the holes at planting time gives some protection.

Pansy are useful in a small garden because they will grow well in light shade. The 'Swiss' or 'Roggli Giant' have large flowers of good texture in separate named colours. For those who prefer a mixture of colours 'Monarch Giant' are very free flowering. A bed of pansy in full bloom under warm sunshine is a cheerfully colourful sight.

Pansy

Petunia

Petunia A half-hardy annual, the petunia offers a colourful selection of varieties. For bedding, the single flowered FI. hybrids are reliable.

Sow the seed in late FEBRUARY, early MARCH in a greenhouse. Pelleted seed may be pressed individually into the surface of the compost, non-pelleted seed is sown very thinly, then just covered with compost. Seedlings are pricked out into boxes or separately into peat pots, hardened off in a frame for planting out during early JUNE. 'Hybrida Multiflora', 8 inches high offers a good range of colours. 'Rose' and 'Red Joy Improved' are promising new varieties in the colour scale, while 'Brass Band' with deep cream flowers and 'Polaris' purple starred white extend the range. 'Blue Skies' is a neat, light blue, but the colour tends to fade. All grow from 6–12 inches high. DO NOT plant in an over manured soil or partial shade. A well drained bed in full sun gives the best results.

A mixed bed of petunia edged with tagetes presents such a gay prospect it almost warms the air above it.

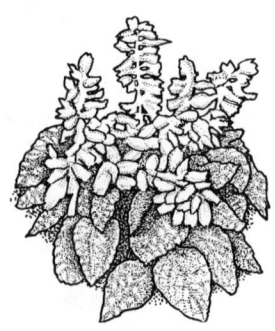

Salvia

Salvia A half-hardy annual, and is important as a bedding plant, but the colour are so startling they should be used with restraint. Some strains will not flower until mid-JULY so it is important to choose an early variety. 'Fire Ball', sometimes known as 'Blaze of Fire', is the best known scarlet – 12 inches. 'Firesprite' is earlier into flower and neater in growth – 10 inches. 'Salmon Pygmy' is dwarfer at 9 inches. Sow the seeds in late FEBRUARY under glass, prick out individually into peat pots then harden off for planting out in early JUNE. A group of scarlet salvia and silver foliaged cineraria against a background of dark shrubs makes a focal point in the garden. A foreground of petunia, 'Brass Band', adds a contrasting cream tone.

Stocks are difficult to place in the garden because of their stiff upright growth. The colour and fragrance of the flowers are an unequalled combination amongst bedding plants. They are grown as half-hardy annuals.

Seed of the Summer flowering or 'ten week' stocks are sown during FEBRUARY in a temperature of 55 degrees F. Prick out after germination into separate peat pots or soil blocks for planting outdoors in the third week in MAY. Height 18 inches, the colours range from yellow through pink to deep mauve. Plant 15 inches apart.

The 'Trysomic Giant Imperial' are taller, up to 20 inches, give 80% double flowers and are useful for bedding and for cutting. Stocks with blocks of aster, 'Milady Rose' and

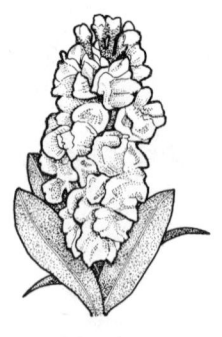

Stock

'Milady Blue' interspersed between make a real cottage garden border.

N.B. When pricking out the 'Trysomic' choose only the strongest seedlings as the less vigorous usually produce single flowers.

Tagetes are half-hardy annuals which have finely divided foliage covered from JUNE onwards with lemon, golden, or crimson flowers, depending on the variety. Sow in mid-MARCH under glass, prick off when large enough to handle into a standard compost 35 to a seed tray. Plant out after hardening off in early JUNE. Seed can also be sown into the open ground where the plants are to flower during late APRIL early MAY.

A bed made up with groups of ageratum 'Blue Blazer', or lobelia and ageratum, makes a neat effective ribbon planting for a narrow border. 'Lemon Gem' brilliant yellow – 7 inches or 'Paprika' crimson are good varieties, especially given a well-drained position in full sun. 'Paprika' can be carpet bedded with lobelia to good effect using pelargoniums as a focal point to the display.

Tagetes

Verbena Unlike the majority of annuals, verbena has spreading growth, so is useful as an edging for taller growing plants or in a window box. Like begonia, most varieties will flower well even in the most miserable Summer weather.

Seeds are sown in peat during MARCH, pricked out three weeks later, then hardened off before transferring outdoors in late MAY.

'Olympia Dwarf Mixed' makes a good 9 inches high multi-coloured carpet under taller growing fuchsia. 'Madame du Barry' is a beautiful deep crimson carmine, taller growing at 12 inches – it can be used as a cut flower.

Annuals can be used to change the character of established shrub borders, to lighten dark corners or for mixing amongst early or late blooming herbaceous plants to give colour in Summer. There are few gardens which could not be made brighter or more interesting by the addition of carefully selected annuals.

Verbena

3 Patio and Tub Plants

Modern housing development frequently includes a flagged patio or paved terrace along one side of the building. The paved area is extremely functional, for usually it is sheltered and private, providing a sitting-out area long before the lawn is fit to use. By the careful siting of tubs and hanging baskets the flagged area ceases to be a bare expanse of stone and can become a prime feature of the garden.

The tubs and containers may be filled with perennial shrubs or herbaceous plants. This is a good policy where there is a large garden to maintain. On a small scale, however, more interesting effects are achieved by changing the planting once or twice a year. There are occasions where only a perennial planting will fill the need. A clematis to cover a bare wall, a camellia in a sheltered, shady alcove, or a magnolia to soften the angle between two walls. All have a place and will grow happily in a tub for many years. Only the house owner can decide which plant design will be most suitable.

A greenhouse, frame or similar window sill is invaluable, for then useful, tender patio plants like pelargoniums, fuchsia, begonia and verbena can be kept from year to year.

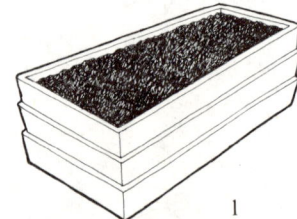

Types of containers

Containers can be had in all shapes or sizes and materials: wood, metal, concrete (1) or moulded plastic. Heavy tubs should be fitted with wheels or castors (2) so they can be moved easily. I find the most economical plant containers are made from beer barrels of various sizes, cut in half and with three or four holes drilled in the bottom (3). Treated with a wood preservative inside and a good coat of paint every two years outside, they will last 20 years. Choose a preservative for treating the wood which will not harm the plants. Not, for example, creosote, which in hot weather can give off fumes which will scorch foliage. Whatever the container is made from: wood, plastic, concrete or stone, there must be holes in the base to provide drainage. Wooden tubs can be drilled as described. The containers cast in concrete or plastic are usually made with holes in the bottom. When the tubs are home made by casting concrete in a mould, wooden plugs can be fitted in the base, then removed as the mixture sets.

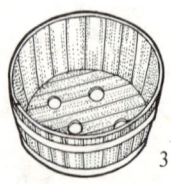

Place a layer of broken clay pot or gravel in the bottom of the tub. On top of this put a covering of course peat, leaf mould or rotten turf to prevent the fine mixture washing down to block the drainage. The actual compost used to fill the tub need not be expensive. A mixture of good garden soil, providing it is weed and disease free, with peat and sand will be suitable. Seven shovelfuls of the soil, four of peat, and enough sand depending on whether the soil is light or heavy to keep the mixture open. To each barrow load of the mixture add a 5-inch pot of John Innes Base fertilizer. This is the fertilizer used in making up the John Innes Potting Compost and is a suitable feed for bedding plants. After 12 months the soil will be impoverished and should be changed. Fill the container, lightly firming the compost as the work proceeds, to within 3 inches of the rim. This allows room for planting and watering. After care includes watering during periods of dry weather, liquid feeding when the plants are into bloom and removal of the dead flower heads.

DESIGN OF A TUB

Choosing the right plants can present problems. Strong, bright colours are best in full sunshine but do draw the eye. Pastel shades lighten the dark corners, looking most attractive when patterned with light and shade.

Fuchsia make very good Summer decoration, flowering over many months with little attention beyond regular watering. They give height to the landscape, particularly if grown on a clean stem instead of a bush (1).

To hang over the sides of the tub the ivy leaved *Pelargonium* (geranium) *peltatum* is attractive both in leaf and flower. 'Blue Peter' has mauve flowers, 'Madam Crousse' double pink and 'L'Elegante' white blossom above delicately marked leaves. When using the white or pink flowered pelargoniums to mask the edge of a tub, trailing lobelia can be alternated with it as a contrast.

1

Composing a picture in a tub or trough is like making up a flower arrangement or painting a landscape. Once the basic outline is in, it almost suggests where the remaining plants should be placed to achieve the best effect. Some petunia left over from the bedding, or even better, special colour forms selected with the tub planting in mind. The F1. select hybrids *Grandiflora petunia* are much better grown in tubs or window boxes than they are in the open garden. The petunia make a second row plant growing to 12 inches. For a position in full sun, 'Astro' with scarlet striped flowers, while in partial shade 'Happiness' with rose pink flowers, would be most suitable.

Both fibrous and tuberous rooted begonia are valuable, providing they are kept well watered. The flowers come in continuous succession over many months. Both can now be grown from seed, then each Autumn the tuberous rooted

varieties are lifted, dried off, and the tubers stored in peat until they are started into growth the following MARCH.

Sow the seed in early MARCH under glass, mixed with sand or brick dust on the surface of a peat based compost, DO NOT cover, just lightly firm. Cover the pots with glass and newspaper, then prick off the seedlings when they are large enough to handle.

Perilla atropurpurea laciniata is useful because it has finely divided bronze purple foliage. Used as a contrast to paler coloured flowers it makes a valuable tub plant, and as it grows up to 24 inches high it should always be used as a centre piece to the tub (1). Seed sown in MARCH under glass will provide plants ready for making up the tubs in JUNE.

Verbena venosa add interest, not so much for the quality of the deep mauve flowers, but because they make such a good foil to the brighter shades of petunia or pelargonium. In the course of a Summer the plants will reach 12 inches, and flowering is continuous. Roots may be lifted each Autumn, overwintered in a cold frame, then either increased from cuttings or by division the following Spring.

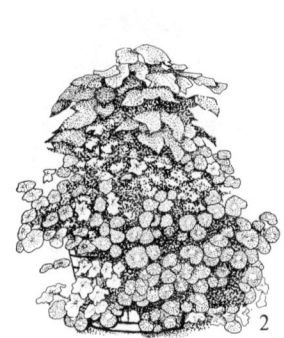

The double flowered orange and red nasturtium *(Tropaeolum majus)*, planted so as to hang over the side of containers with the dark flowered verbena behind, make an effective association (2). Seeds of the nasturtium 'Gleam Strain' are sown in a frame during MARCH, then potted up singly for growing on.

The dwarf forms of *Cineraria maritima* with grey foliage are effective as a foil, indeed, foliage plants play an important part in any bedding scheme. Seed of the variety 'Silver Dust' or the taller 'Diamond' sown in a greenhouse in early MARCH would give strong, well-foliaged plants for tub planting in JUNE. They are effective in association with scarlet begonia or orange red flowered pelargonium.

Because of their long flowering season the low growing antirrhinums 'Coronette' and 'Floral Cluster' are splendid patio and terrace garden material. The upright, sturdy growth needing no support means they can be used in the less sheltered areas, possibly with an edging of the copper or yellow marigolds. Seed should be sown as for bedding in FEBRUARY or MARCH into a peat based compost. The marigolds are sown in mid-MARCH to be just in flower by early JUNE when they can be planted into the containers. Any of the varieties of marigold from 6 inches up to 18 inches are suitable for tub or container culture.

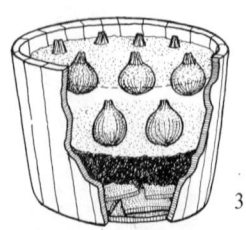

Once the Summer bedding has been cleared, the tubs and troughs may be planted up with bulbs (3), wallflowers, polyanthus, primroses, violas. A different scheme may be tried each year – dark red hyacinths with pale blue viola – polyanthus, one of the dark red hybrids with yellow tulips. Another most effective combination is lavender tulips with creamy yellow polyanthus. Choice of colour scheme depends on personal taste, and the degree of light or shade in which the container will be sited.

By growing dwarf shrubs in pots (azalea, *Prunus cistena* or coloured foliaged conifers), then plunging them, still in the pot, into the tubs, miniature landscapes may be built up. Snowdrops, dwarf narcissii and tulips or scilla 'Spring Beauty' can be used to make up a Spring display. As the flowers fade, the bulbs are lifted and potted up or heeled in until required the following year. This method saves an annual expenditure of several pounds.

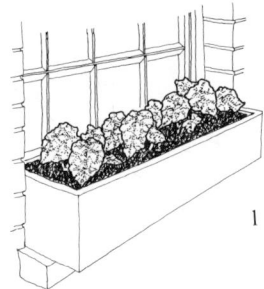

HANGING BASKET

Any patio garden can be improved if the wall of the house is decorated with a window box (1) and a hanging basket which are a feature in themselves.

Window boxes are bedded out in very much the same way as a tub or trough. Hanging baskets need more care. First make sure the hook put in to hang the basket from is capable of supporting the weight. A basket weighing up to a stone could be very unpleasant dropped onto an unprotected head from several feet up.

The basket is first lined with good quality sphagnum moss (2); binding or weaving the material so the wire framework is hidden. When time permits, choose a selection of trailing plants such as lobelia or nasturtium which can actually be planted through the base of the basket, so that even from beneath only flowers are visible. Fill the basket with good quality compost with some lumps of charcoal added to keep the mixture sweet. Plants in peat pots may be plunged directly into this (3). Hanging baskets need regular feeding and watering to keep the plants in healthy condition – without the charcoal a compost would become sour.

Once again, the begonia are in the forefront of useful plants for filling a hanging basket (4), particularly the *B. lloydii*. Mixed seed can be bought from any major seedsmen and germinated in a temperature of 65 degrees F.

The ivy leaved pelargoniums, previously described, are trained to hang over the edge of a basket and will flower continuously throughout the Summer.

The trailing varieties of lobelia 'Blue Basket', 'Red

Cascade' and 'Blue Cascade' have been expressly developed as an edging for baskets or window boxes. Sow the seed in a heated place during MARCH.

Campanula isophylla is a trailing perennial easily raised from cuttings; the trailing growth and continuous flowering make it very suitable for basket work. The blue, or in the variety *alba,* white flowers almost mask the leaves from JULY onwards. Cuttings of non-flowering side or basal shoots taken in MAY to JUNE root easily when inserted in sharp sand.

Trailing forms of nasturtium *(Tropaeolum majus)* will flower well, planted in baskets. Sow the seed as for tub planting during MARCH in a frame to give plants large enough for transplanting into the basket in late MAY.

Asparagus sprengeri compactus, because of the lovely foliage and pendulous habit, may also be included. Increase the plants by division in mid-MARCH. Though seed can be sown in APRIL it will be a year before seedlings can be used for the baskets.

Almost all the upright growing plants suitable for cultivation in tubs or containers will do well in hanging baskets. Zonal pelargoniums, petunias, fuchsia varieties like 'Cascade', 'Falling Stars' or 'Golden Marinka', marigolds and the bedding calceolaria will provide a good display of colour.

The fuchsia should be propagated from cuttings of non-flowering shoots taken during the Summer to provide strong young plants the following year. Cuttings of pelargoniums taken in SEPTEMBER to OCTOBER of short non-flowering shoots, 3 inches long, then overwintered under cover will be a suitable size for planting in baskets the following MAY.

Calceolaria, particularly the FI. hybrid 'Sunshine', are extremely free flowering. Stock raised from seed sown in late FEBRUARY, early MARCH, will have grown sufficiently large enough to plant up in baskets in mid-MAY.

Once the various plants are in position to achieve the best effect, mask all the bare earth with a further layer of sphagnum moss. Before hanging the basket in its permanent position, keep it in a lower, sheltered place so that watering and training can be attended to daily. When the plants are well established, regular watering and feeding, every ten days is all that is necessary.

Positioning the basket is important, in a porch or french window, above a garage or front door, or in spaces between windows at the front of a house.

4 House and Pot Plants

House plants enable people without a plot of land to enjoy gardening. The cultivation of a begonia or cyclamen on a kitchen windowsill can bring the same satisfaction that the gardener with half an acre derives from growing a magnolia or a rose outdoors.

Some of the plants which are grown in pots have only a brief season of beauty. Azalea, cyclamen, primula and cineraria are only attractive when in flower. Most are difficult to keep in healthy growth except under greenhouse conditions, so are brought into the house when in flower, and as the flowers fade, are taken back to the greenhouse to recuperate. Others are 'house plants' and are capable of surviving in the house the whole year round. Sansevieria (Mother-in-law's Tongue), aspidistra and chlorophytum are examples of pot plants which adapt easily to average living room conditions.

All house plants will put up with considerable variation in temperature and atmospheric moisture. Extremes, which so frequently occur in the living room – 80 to 85 degrees F during the afternoon or evening falling to near freezing by dawn, are not good for even the toughest house plant. The dry air found in many centrally heated buildings will kill most plants. Leaves lose moisture quicker than the roots, no matter how well the plant is watered. This problem can be overcome by standing the pot on a tray of pebbles, peat or similar absorbant material which is kept saturated with water (1). Evaporation from the tray keeps the air around the plant moist preventing the leaves drying out.

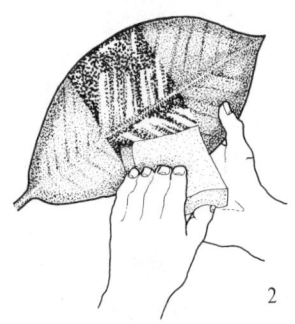

Watering must still be attended to even if the plant is standing on a tray. When the soil starts to dry out, give the root ball a thorough soaking by plunging the pot up to its rim in a bowl of water. Once the air bubbles stop bursting on top of the compost it is well and truly saturated.

Light is also an important essential for maintaining plants in good health. Direct sunlight will do no harm providing the roots are kept moist, but good indirect light will suit most plants as they do not then dry out so quickly. Avoid dense shade as it encourages weak, spindly growth.

The large leaved plants, for example the rubber plant (ficus), become dusty and do not function efficiently. A sponge down with tepid water twice a week will keep them in condition (2).

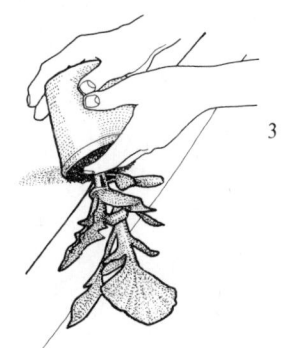

Re-potting will be necessary even when the plants are fed regularly. To test, press the compost at the top of the pot with the fingers, when it is packed with roots it is time to repot. Knock out the plant (3) by turning the container upside down, then with the fingers of one hand spread out

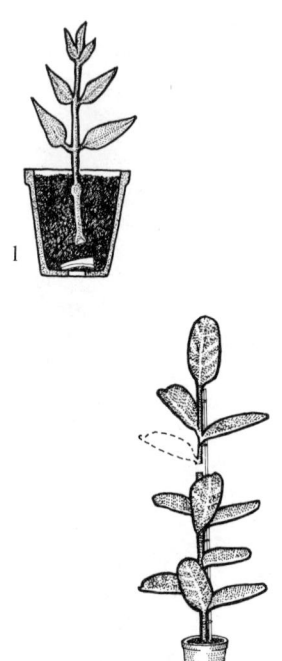

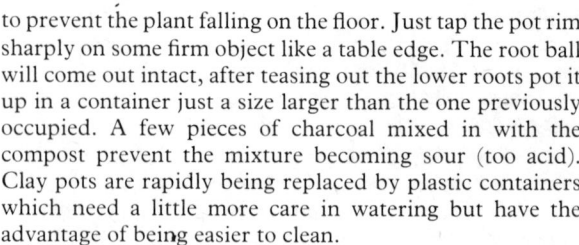

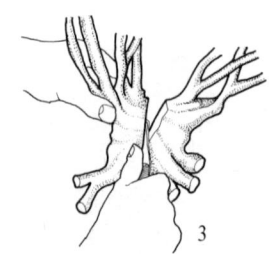

to prevent the plant falling on the floor. Just tap the pot rim sharply on some firm object like a table edge. The root ball will come out intact, after teasing out the lower roots pot it up in a container just a size larger than the one previously occupied. A few pieces of charcoal mixed in with the compost prevent the mixture becoming sour (too acid). Clay pots are rapidly being replaced by plastic containers which need a little more care in watering but have the advantage of being easier to clean.

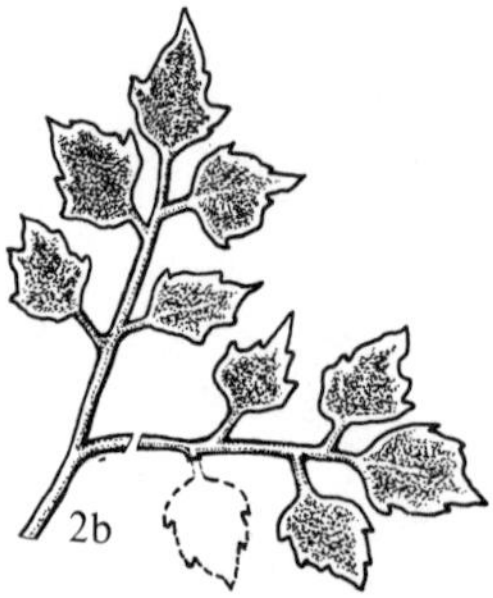

Composts based on peat are replacing to some extent the traditional soil-based John Innes mixtures. Plants potted in peat mixtures must never be short of water and will need feeding at fortnightly intervals once the roots are established, usually a month after potting.

Problems of dry air, draughts, fluctuating temperatures apply equally in the greenhouse. Indeed, the basic cultivations are the same whether the subject is a pot or true house plant.

Sometimes the necessity of complete repotting can be overcome by removing carefully the top layer of compost from a pot and replacing it with a fresh mixture. Care must be taken with this method that no surface roots are damaged.

PROPAGATION

Most indoor plants are readily increased from cuttings. Some, like the 'Busy Lizzie', will root if the shoots are just cut, then stood upright in a tumbler of water. The best rooting medium is sharp sand, this is placed in a 4-inch diameter half pot. Cuttings of the plant to be propagated are taken, dipped in rooting powder and dibbled into the pot (1). To ensure they do not dry out, cover them with a polythene bag secured to the pot with an elastic band. A small propagator with a heated base covered with a transparent lid is even more effective in providing the right conditions for cuttings.

Cuttings are made from the tips of shoots when the plants have a distinct stem and branches, for example rubber plant (2a), ivy (2b) or coleus.

Division is practical when a plant forms several crowns and can be split up into sections each with a terminal shoot (3), for example *Begonia rex* or *Maranta*.

Leaf cuttings Some of the pot and house plants with fleshy leaves may be increased by removing healthy leaves, inserting them in sandy compost, where in due course they develop roots – African violet and Mother-in-law's Tongue are examples. Leaf cuttings can also be made with *Begonia rex* by removing a leaf, cutting across the main veins, then pegging it down flat on a sand base (1). Young plants grow from the cut area. With African violets pull off young leaves with a stalk, then dibble them around the edge of a pot in sharp sand. A young plant will form at the leaf base. For Mother-in-law's Tongue, select healthy young leaves and chop them into sections. Each section can be persuaded to root if one end is pushed into a sandy compost.

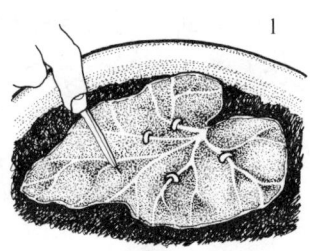

Pruning with most of the house plants is limited to the removal of the dead flower heads as they fade.

DISPLAY

How the pot or house plants are displayed depends on the type of plant and design of room. Too many individual pots dotted about a room make a lot of work. Grouped together in one of the trough-shaped containers, available in a wide variety of designs, they are much more effective and take less looking after. Troughs with solid sides can be filled with peat and the pots plunged into that, which cuts down the watering (2).

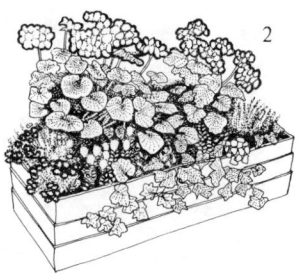

Hanging baskets suspended from a window, alcove or hall make a pleasant decoration.

Where a wall space is available, pot holders may be fitted to the walls and filled with climbing plants. Some of the shoots may be allowed to hang down naturally, while others can be trained up onto a wood or metal trellis.

The modern version of the Victorian Wardian case is a practical way of growing plants in rooms with a very dry atmosphere (3). The case is a greenhouse in miniature with a thermostatically controlled heating element. Attractive groupings of even the more difficult house plants can be made in these. The conditions provided suit the Saintpaulia (African violet) which, though extremely attractive, is not easy to keep healthy.

The glass carboy or bottle garden (4) is a recent extension of the same idea. Containers of this type must be thoroughly cleaned first, and then allowed to dry. The compost must not be too rich, otherwise the carboy soon becomes filled with leaves. A few pieces of charcoal in the base of the container will help keep the mixture sweet (on the lime side of neutral).

Suitable plants for a bottle or carboy garden are *Cryptanthus bivittatus*, *Pteris cretica*, *Ficus pumila*, certain

Aphelandra

Beloperone

Citrus

Cyclamen

hedera (ivy), sansevieria and maranta. Care must be taken not to over water the bottle garden, and if the container is corked after the initial watering no more should be needed for several weeks. DO NOT stand the container in direct sunlight.

Landscapes in miniature can be created by choosing plants of contrasting heights and leafshapes, or sculpting the soil with pieces of ornamental stone.

PLANTS WITH FLOWERS OR FRUIT

Aphelandra squarrosa 'Louisae' Dual purpose plant, foliage dark green striped white – tubular yellow flowers in late Summer. Height 18 inches (young side shoots which grow from leaf joints when the dead flower is cut away root readily in peat and sand compost).

Beloperone guttata (Shrimp Plant) – brown, pink and yellow bracts up to 6 inches long open from Spring until Autumn. Height 20 inches. Keep shaded from direct sunlight. (Cuttings of non-flowering shoots taken at any time during the growing season are quite easy to root.)

Citrus mitis makes a most attractive pot and house plant. The intensely fragrant flowers are followed by small tangerine orange like fruits. A fairly high temperature is required to ripen the fruit – 60 degrees F. Citrus frequently show magnesium deficiency – a teaspoonful of Epsom salts to a gallon of water will correct this. Height 24 inches, but plants flower and fruit when only 8 inches high.

Cyclamen is a deservedly popular flowering pot plant. Some varieties, for example *Cyclamen persicum rex* have attractively marbled leaves as well as beautiful flowers. The blooming period is from SEPTEMBER onwards throughout the Winter months. Maintain a temperature of 55 degrees F and keep in full light. To ensure a humid atmosphere, place the pot on a block of wood standing in a bowl filled with water. Liquid feeding should commence as the flower buds open, and continue at 14 day intervals. DO NOT throw the plant (corm) away as the flowers fade, but stop feeding and gradually reduce the water until the soil is dry. The pot can stand outside during the Summer with a piece of glass over to keep out the rain. In AUGUST start growth again by watering, then repot into fresh compost.

Seed sown in JANUARY will grow to flowering size plants by the following DECEMBER.

Fuchsia are not in the top flight of house plants, but are very good value in the greenhouse or bedded out during the Summer with the annuals. Indoors they grow best in a cool airy room: dry air causes the flowers to drop, so keep well watered and liquid feed every 14 days. Cuttings of short side growths root easily in sand.

Hydrangea Cuttings are rooted into a sandy compost, potted into 3-inch pots then grown on until large enough to pot on into 6-inch pots where they are to flower. Use an acid compost for blue flowered varieties. Rest the plants in a cold frame before starting them into growth for flowers to appear from MARCH onwards. Cool, moist air and freedom from draughts will prolong the flowering season. Liquid feed every 14 days.

Impatiens The ever popular 'Busy Lizzie' with white, pink, red or orange flowers requires plenty of moisture during the growing period, the supply being reduced during the Winter. Tip cuttings, 4 inches long, if taken during the Summer root readily into a sand compost. As the plants develop, pinch out the growing tip to keep a bushy habit. Repot each year in MARCH and liquid feed every 3 weeks during the Summer.

Poinsettia Because the brightly coloured bracts which surround the flowers hold their colour for several months, poinsettia are good value as house plants. Deep crimson is the most popular colour but there are forms available with white, pink, or bright scarlet bracts. A temperature of 55 degrees F is quite suitable, providing the atmosphere is not dry. A liquid feed every 16 days to 21 days will keep the plant healthy. Young leaves scorch if exposed to hot Summer sunshine, so, as bracts fade, allow the pots to dry out, then in MARCH cut the bracts hard back to provide young shoots as cuttings. These root in sand. To prevent the sticky sap oozing out dip the wound in charcoal and then rooting powder.

Schlumbergera (Zygocactus) prefer a light, humus rich soil – 2 parts loam, 2 parts peat, 1 part sand with a dusting of bone meal – ½ oz to every 5 lb of compost. A humid atmosphere and light position are essential (West or East facing windowsill) with adequate moisture during the growing season. Liquid feed every 10 days as the buds form. DO NOT allow the soil to dry out or the buds drop. Cuttings of the flattened stems taken at a joint will root better if the wound is allowed to heal before inserting them

Fuchsia

Hydrangea

Impatiens

Poinsettia

Schlumbergera

in a sandy compost. After flowering, stand the pots outdoors during the Summer to rest – they still need water in dry weather.

Solanum capsicastrum (Winter Cherry). A neat little shrub with dark green leaves. The small white flowers are followed by round fruits which ripen through shades of orange to scarlet during Autumn and Winter. Cuttings potted up in John Innes No 2 or peat-based compost should stand in a frame during Summer. Leading shoots are kept pinched to make the plants bush out. Syringe over daily to help the flowers set. Liquid feed every 10 days adding a teaspoonful of Epsom salts to every gallon of water to mix with every second feed. This corrects any shortage of magnesium. Bring the pots indoors in SEPTEMBER to a light airy position, moist air and a temperature of 50–55 degrees F. High temperatures cause both the berries and leaves to drop.

Solanum

FOLIAGE HOUSE AND POT PLANTS

Begonia rex Given the conditions which suit it, *Begonia rex* makes a beautiful house plant. A correct atmosphere is more easily maintained in a greenhouse where full beauty of leaf is achieved. Keep the pots moist when cultivating them in the home, this stops the roots drying out and improves the humidity. Dry air or gas heating can damage the leaves – 55 to 60 degrees F during the Winter months is ideal. Liquid feed at fortnight intervals from MAY to AUGUST. Under greenhouse conditions some shade may be needed in the Summer. The leaves can measure up to 15 inches across and are attractively patterned in silver, bronze, purple or pink. Propagation is by leaf cuttings of mature but not old leaves, cut across the veins and peg down flat on a sandy compost. Height 15 inches.

Begonia

Chlorophytum elatum 'Variegatum' is one of the most accommodating of pot plants. A position away from direct sunlight, or which only catches the sun in late afternoon, such as a West facing window sill, is the best. The John Innes No 1 or peat based composts are suitable. The 12 inch long grass-like leaves are pale green banded with white, and young plantlets grow on the ends of long runners. A Winter temperature of 45 degrees F is adequate. Keep well watered during the Summer – reduce the supply from OCTOBER to MARCH. The young plantlets may be pegged down into small pots and rooted.

Chlorophytum

Coleus Has nettle like leaves coloured in various shades of red, purple, yellow and green. Seeds sown in JANUARY will grow into plants showing a wide variation in leaf colour, the best of these can be propagated by cuttings made from healthy young shoots in MARCH. Any flowers which develop should be nipped out immediately they appear to keep the plant in shape. Water regularly in Summer, keep on the dry side in Winter. Liquid feed at 3 week intervals from APRIL to SEPTEMBER. Keep the plants in good light or growth becomes spindly.

Coleus

Dracaena are grown for their beautifully striped or marbled foliage. They need the maximum light, particularly in Winter, to ensure full development of the partly coloured leaves. A fairly rich compost is required. John Innes No 2 or a peat-based mixture plus a liquid feed once every 3 weeks from MAY to SEPTEMBER. A Winter temperature of 50 degrees F is satisfactory. Tip cuttings, basal growths or pieces of old stem cut into sections will all root inserted in sand, given a temperature of 65 degrees F.

Dracaena

x **Fatshedera lizei** (Fat-headed Lizzie) is a house plant with the advantage that when it has grown too large to be accommodated indoors it can be planted out in the garden. The dark shining evergreen leaves are deeply lobed, and, in the form *Variegata*, marked with creamy white. Cuttings made from shoot tips are not hard to root in sandy compost. Tolerant of poor light and cooler conditions, fatshedera make admirable decoration for a hall or stairway so long as there are no vicious draughts to discolour the leaves. Height up to 4 feet or more in the open garden.

Fatshedera

Ficus elastica decora (India Rubber Plant). The dark glossy green leaves up to 12 inches in length are a most decorative feature. Dry air causes the lower leaves to turn yellow and drop off, so keep well watered and humid at all times. Propagation is possible by air layers – make a shallow cut in the stem about 2 inches long, paint the wound with rooting powder using a match stalk to hold the cut surfaces apart. Pack round the cut with moist sphagnum moss held in place with a polythene sleeve and sealed at the top and bottom with electricians tape to make it water tight. The sleeve is left in position until the roots are visible through the moss, the cutting is then detached and potted up in the normal way. 'Doescheri' and 'Tricolor' have variegated leaves. In Winter a temperature of 62 degrees F is best. Repot annually into a slightly larger pot during APRIL. Liquid feed every ten days from MAY to SEPTEMBER.

Ficus

Hedera

Maranta

Sansevieria

Hedera Varieties of the common ivy are very suitable for indoor pot culture. Some have large leaves attractively variegated, others are crinkled or narrowly pointed but all dislike hot, dry conditions. They prefer humid, slightly cooler air and a position away from direct sunlight. All forms of ivy seem to do better if trained upright instead of being allowed to hang down. Cuttings 3–4 inches long made from the ends of shoots will root in moist sand or even a jar of water.

Varieties of common ivy *(Hedera helix)* are 'Buttercup', 'Discolor' (marbled leaves) and 'Silver Queen' (leaves tinged pink in Winter).

Repot every other year in APRIL. Keep moist but not too wet, and liquid feed every 3 weeks.

Maranta leuconeura Contains several varieties with pleasing foliage for cultivation as a pot plant. *M. kerchoveana* has apple green leaves with brown or purple markings, sometimes known as the 'Prayer Plant' because the leaves stand upright and together at night. *M. massangeana* (Fishbone Plant) has dark green leaves with veins marked with white.

All prefer warm humid air, growing best under greenhouse or bottle garden conditions. Because they grow fairly quickly repotting may be necessary twice a year into John Innes No 2 compost or a proprietary peat-based mixture. Liquid feed every 14 days will prevent the plants becoming starved. Mature plants should be divided and replanted in APRIL. Hot dry conditions may cause top growth to die right back, but if the pots are moved into a humid atmosphere usually new shoots will sprout.

Sansevieria trifasciata, popularly known as 'Mother-in-law's Tongue' are desert plants. The upright, twisted sword like leaves are mottled grey green and margined with a band of yellow in the form *Laurentii*. Being desert plants they need a gritty, well drained soil – John Innes compost with an extra part of sand to every three parts of the mixture will be suitable. Water sparingly in Winter, particularly if the plants are kept in a fairly low temperature 50 to 55 degrees F. No more than once a month in Winter, but about every 10 days in Summer if the weather is hot and dry.

Repot every 3 years. Slice the leaves into 2-inch pieces, then press into moist sand so the base is buried $\frac{1}{2}$-inch deep. The form *Laurentii* can only be propagated by the division of young growths (suckers) from the base of the parent plant.

Zebrina pendula is a trailing plant with leaves marked silver on green above, purple on the undersides. They are very suitable for growing in wall containers or hanging baskets above a window. A light, airy position away from direct sunlight, with adequate water during the growing season plus a liquid feed every 3 weeks will keep the plants in healthy condition. Repotting each year in APRIL is suitable. Winter temperature 50 to 55 degrees F is advisable. Tip cuttings 3–4 inches long root readily in moist sand.

Zebrina

PROBLEMS WITH HOUSE AND GREENHOUSE PLANTS

Greenfly are easily controlled with one of the proprietory insecticides. A systemic poison which is taken up into the sapstream of the plant is suitable, remaining active for up to 6 weeks.

Leaf hoppers feed on the undersides of leaves causing mottling. Spraying with Lindane repeated 10 days later should give a control.

Red spider by feeding on the leaves causes yellowing of the tissue. Regular syringing with tepid water and spraying with derris liquid reduces the pest.

Whitefly weaken the plants by feeding on all the green parts, they also deposit a sticky substance which renders the foliage unsightly. Spray with malathion at 14 day intervals until signs of infestation are cleared up.

Mealy bug Tufts of waxy wool indicate the presence of this pest – look particularly in leaf axils or crowns of the plants. Painting with methylated spirits or watering with a systemic insecticide will clear up the trouble.

Scale insects A systemic insecticide clears the nuisance or paint the colonies with a malathion solution.

Disease

Grey mould – best prevented by keeping a buoyant atmosphere, avoid overcrowding or excess moisture. Spray infected plants with captan or fumigate in a greenhouse with tecnazene.

Magnesium deficiency – a condition indicated by yellowing foliage – water with a teaspoonful of Epsom salts to a gallon of water.

Mildew Control by keeping the air fresh and buoyant. Sulphur dusts are a control, once infection is apparent.

5 The Mixed Border

Modern housing development and the continuing increase in the price of building land inevitably means smaller gardens. There is just not the space to keep shrubs, herbaceous plants and bulbs separate, and so they are all combined into a mixed border.

The owner of a new garden has only the problem of deciding what to grow and where. Difficulties arise when the garden has already been planted then neglected. Consider which features are to be pulled out or moved to a new position. Possibly a tree, planted in ignorance of the amount of space it will occupy in maturity, threatens to take over the whole garden. Trees take years to grow and only hours to uproot, so irreversible decisions of this sort should not be made in a hurry. Live with the garden for a while, look at the permanent features such as trees and shrubs, find out if they will play a part in the proposed new design. Only then start in with spade, secateurs and saw, stepping back at intervals as work proceeds to make certain nothing valuable is being removed. Whatever trees and shrubs are retained they will probably need pruning. This should be done before any digging or other similar pre-planting work is begun – assuming, of course, it is the right time of the year. In Autumn, cut out dead, diseased or crossing branches, then paint all the wounds with Stockholm tar or similar antiseptic water repellant.

One of the most time consuming tasks in the garden is that of weeding, so make sure that perennial weeds like ground elder, couch or convolvulus are killed out before planting takes place. The soil should be forked over and a dressing of organic matter, peat, well rotted manure or compost mixed in at the same time. The fertility of the soil is maintained with a mulch of the same materials each year after the planting is completed. In Spring, just as growth commences apply a complete fertilizer dressing at the rate of 2 oz per sq. yard. A weed-free, moisture-retentive, fertile soil is the gardener's best insurance against disease.

The shape of a mixed border is important, viewed both from, and in relationship to, the house. If the border is sheltered by a hedge, make certain surface roots will not compete with newly introduced shrubs. Long curving lines leading away from the house express an invitation to walk round a garden. Possibly a tree provides shade which can be utilized to protect tender shrubs from frost, or moisture loving plants from the Summer sun. The pattern of light and shade through the branches of a tree falling onto pale coloured flowers underneath is a pleasant prospect on a bright Summer day. Every factor must be noted and used particularly in the limited space of a small garden.

Having decided how many of the existing plants must be left, then clean and prepare the soil so the remaining spaces can be filled. When there is a gap between two houses this creates a draughty tunnel, so the shrub opposite that must be carefully selected.

Acer palmatum 'Atro-purpureum' the red Japanese Maple – superb in form and leaf, is a key element in the design of a border. The best effect is achieved when the maple is sited so that from the house it is seen with the conifer and cherry in the foreground. On the shady side of the maple plant some white flowered Daffodil 'Mount Hood'.

Aconitum wilsonii 'Barkers Variety', tall growing monkshood, has dark purple flowers in late Summer and Autumn. Because it grows 6 feet high, it should be kept to the back of the border. It is a herbaceous perennial.

Anthemis tinctoria is found growing wild in many parts of Britain. A herbaceous perennial, it will grow in most soils which are well drained with an open aspect, and flowers profusely throughout the Summer. The most reliable variety is the lemon flowered 'Mrs Buxton' which grows 24 inches high.

Aquilegia are amongst the most popular border plants. Sow seed of the 'Long Spurred Hybrids' in a frame or nursery border in early MAY. Transfer to the open garden in Spring the following year to flower in early Summer.

Berberis thunbergii 'Rose Glow' is a colourful shrub small enough to fit neatly into the smaller garden. The young leaves are attractively mottled with white and rose on dark purple. Just the dark contrast for a potentilla when viewed from the house. A shrub for either acid or lime soil, which also colours attractively in the Autumn.

Berberis x stenophylla is tall enough to protect the rest of the border and tough enough to stand the wind. It is bone hardy, will grow 7 feet high, and makes a thicket of evergreen foliage covered by fragrant yellow flowers in Spring.

Campanula carpatica A perennial with cup-shaped blue flowers is in truth an alpine, but grows contentedly in any well-drained soil. Only 6 inches high, both the white and blue varieties are worth a place in the most select border.

Acer

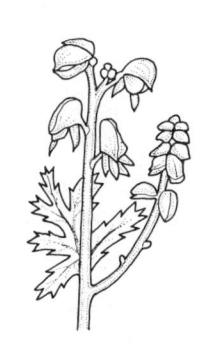

Aconitum

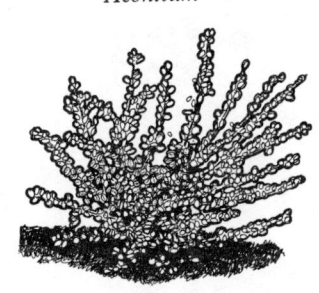

Berberis

Campanula

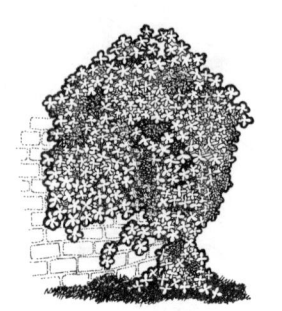

Clematis, a climber which can often be supported by established trees. Deep rooted subjects like the oak (*quercus*) are ideal for this purpose as there is scarcely any root competition. The type of clematis chosen depends on the support; a forest tree like the 'oak' or 'Scots pine' will carry *Clematis montana* with ease. In Spring the pink or white scented flowers make a curtain of colour. Less vigorous trees, Crab apple or Cherry will support a 'Perle d'Azur' or a 'Markhams Pink'.

Cotoneaster 'Hybridus Pendulus' is a handsome prostrate evergreen, excellent for taking the hard edge off a path or growing on a sloping bank. The red fruits in Autumn contrast with the dark green leaves. When grown as a standard on a 5-foot stem, it makes a first class weeping tree for the small garden. Like all cotoneasters, it is not too discerning in regard to soil or climate.

Delphinium A herbaceous perennial which provides a change in shape, the upright flower spikes opening in JUNE, JULY and AUGUST are superb. They can be grown from seed sown in frames during APRIL to flower 18 months later. Alternatively, named varieties enable colour schemes to be planned more exactly. Young growth from the roots should be reduced to 3, 5 or 7 as they break in Spring. The remainder will then produce fuller, better formed spikes on strong 6 to 8-foot stems.

Deutzia x magnificata is equally hardy but loses its foliage in Winter, the double white flowers open in JULY. A shrub which can be used to block a draught between two buildings to give shelter to more tender plants.

Dianthus the perennial 'Cottage Pinks' can be raised from seed, the grey foliage and sweetly scented flowers bring a singular beauty to the border. A hot, dry fairly arid soil suits them best, so choose a position in full sun. Seed may be sown in FEBRUARY under glass or in a nursery border during early MAY.

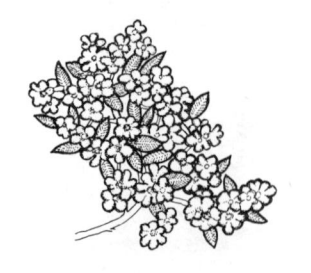

Escallonia 'Donard Radiance' is an evergreen which starts to blossom in MAY and continues throughout the Summer. Individual blooms are comparatively large and rose red. Nearly all escallonia are remarkably tolerant of pruning. 'Donard Radiance' is no exception and can be cut hard back after the first flush of flowers. Evergreen shrubs with a long flowering season are uncommon, which is why the smaller members of the genus escallonia are so valuable.

Clematis

Delphinium

Escallonia

Fuchsia 'Mrs. Popple' provides the Autumn colour. It gives a succession of blue and red flowers from AUGUST until the frost. Pruned back to soil level in APRIL, it will never grow much above 3 feet high and can spread up to 6 feet wide. It can be planted in partial shade or full sun, and prefers a well-nourished soil. It is advisable, especially in the North, to protect the roots in Winter.

Hebe speciosa hybrids are tender shrubs which may be cultivated outdoors. They are liable to damage in exposed situations but given a little shelter, which so many suburban gardens provide, they will not only survive but grow to 4 feet tall and flower well into Winter. The glossy green leaves and rich red flowers of Hebe 'Simon Deleaux' are an asset to any garden.

Helenium autumnale 'Crimson Beauty' is a useful herbaceous perennial to fill the gaps and give height to the border while the shrubs are growing in. The copper red flowers on 3-foot stems need full sun to bring out all the glowing richness of the colour.

Hosta fortunei 'Albopicta' has bright yellow and green leaves. Growing 18 inches high, it continues the theme of continuing colour. Hosta are a lot more tolerant of dry weather than was at first supposed, but a cool, moist soil suits them best.

Hydrangea 'Veitchii' ('Lace Cap'). A shrub with white flowers, which in contradiction then fade to deep pink, will be best suited in the shade offered by the house or taller growing shrubs.

Hypericum x inodorum 'Elstead' looks most elegant when patterned with the play of sunlight through overhanging trees, and fortunately is quite tolerant of partial shade. Eventually it will grow into a bush 4 feet high with pale yellow flowers, followed in due season by salmon red fruits. Most soils are acceptable so long as they are reasonably well drained.

Juniperus x media 'Old Gold' is a low growing conifer whose young shoots open bronze gold, the colour persisting throughout the Winter. In nine years it will grow 3 feet high by about 4 feet across and will contrast, say, with the vertical line of the cherry. To fill the gap between the cherry and conifer plant some narcissus 'Peeping Tom' which have deep golden flowers on 8-inch stems during MARCH.

Helenium

Hypericum

Juniperus

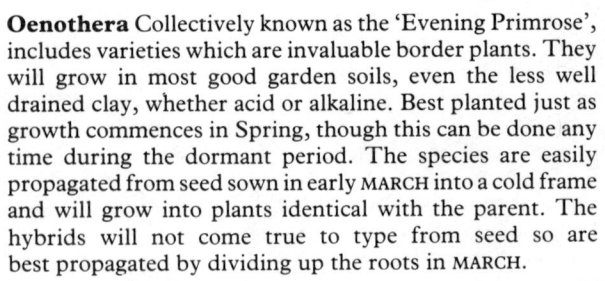

Oenothera Collectively known as the 'Evening Primrose', includes varieties which are invaluable border plants. They will grow in most good garden soils, even the less well drained clay, whether acid or alkaline. Best planted just as growth commences in Spring, though this can be done any time during the dormant period. The species are easily propagated from seed sown in early MARCH into a cold frame and will grow into plants identical with the parent. The hybrids will not come true to type from seed so are best propagated by dividing up the roots in MARCH.

Suitable hybrids are 'Fireworks' red buds, deep yellow flowers and 12 to 15 inches high, and 'Highlight' bright yellow.

Species – O.missouriensis only 6 inches high but with enormous yellow flowers throughout the Summer.

Phlox are herbaceous plants of high Summer which prefer a cool moist soil, so work a shovelful of wet peat around the roots at planting time. Because phlox are cottage garden flowers, where space is limited mix the colours and heights – three 'Otley Purple' 18 inches high with violet flowers, or 'Prince of Orange' orange red, and, to soften the effect, two 'Mai Ruys' equally dwarf, but with pure white flowers.

Pieris formosa 'Forrestii', like rhododendron, needs an acid soil. Even a mere hint of lime turns them yellow and sickly. In the northern areas of the British Isles, pieris needs some protection, though usually the over-hanging branches of a taller shrub or small tree are sufficient. In Spring when the dark evergreen leaves are a background to the white flowers and scarlet young growths, this is one of the loveliest pictures a garden affords. Keep the bushes well watered in dry weather and a mulch of peat over the roots. Snowdrops look beautiful planted in groups around the pieris.

Platycodon grandiflorum mariesii, the unusual 'Chinese Bellflower', a herbaceous perennial whose large cup shaped blue flowers are evident from JULY to SEPTEMBER is worth a place. Enjoying the same cool, humus rich soil as the phlox, the tallest stems rarely top 12 inches in height, which makes it a useful plant for the border front. Sow the seed in a sheltered bed outdoors and let them grow on there for 18 months. Then transplant to the border. Platycodon are difficult to propagate successfully by division, and this should be attempted before the plants are 4 years old.

Potentilla fruticosa hybrids are shrubs which will flower right through the Summer and this is why they are so valuable. The variety 'Moonlight' will grow 3 feet high and produce a succession of soft primrose yellow flowers from MAY to OCTOBER. Any soil whether acid or lime is suitable and it thrives in sun or light shade.

Prunus 'Amanogawa' can be used to flank the path and frame the view from the house. It is a small, completely upright cherry with clusters of semi-double pink blossom in Spring. Height about 18 feet, spread 6 feet, an excellent tree where space is limited.

Pulsatilla vulgaris the 'Pasque Flower' is attractive in both foliage and flower. Growth is neat, up to 12 inches high, which makes it suitable for even a very small mixed border. The grey green foliage is finely divided and almost fern like. The buds are covered on the outside with silver hairs and open to cup shaped flowers with a central cone of yellow stamens. Colour range is from cream, dark purple, lavender, pink and deep red. Seed may be sown immediately it is ripe in JULY into boxes filled with John Innes compost or one of the peat based mixtures. DO NOT bury the seed too deeply or it will not germinate. Prick off the seedlings before they become overcrowded and plant out 12 months after sowing in a well drained soil, apply a mulch of compost or peat. Chalk soil is the natural habitat of the Pulsatilla, but they succeed as well in an acid or chalk mixture.

Rhododendron 'Praecox' continues the theme of colour all the year round, and in a mild Winter will start to open purple crimson buds in FEBRUARY. Growth is compact up to 4 feet, but like all rhododendrons, an acid soil is essential. Underneath, a group of blue and white crocus will gradually naturalise to carpet the ground and flower at the same time.

Salvia nemerosa 'Lubeca' contrasts with the yellow flowers of the potentilla. It is a herbaceous, perennial plant with grey green leaves and dark purple flowers.

Santolina chamaecyparissus, the silver foliaged 'Lavender Cotton', a perennial, which bears pom-pom heads of lemon flowers on foot high stems in JULY and AUGUST, may be used as ground cover below the monkshood *(Aconitum wilsonii)*. A garden to be worthy of the name should have an all the year round interest.

Potentilla

Prunus

Santolina

Sedum

Trollius

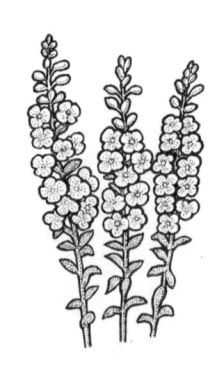

Veronica

Sedum spectabile 'Brilliant' is 12 inches high, a glaucous-leaved herbaceous plant, which becomes a mound of deep rose magenta flowers in SEPTEMBER. With its grey green leaves, it can be used as a foil to the helenium, and in a long narrow border it is a good idea to repeat a group of it at intervals.

Trollius 'Earliest of All' enjoys the shade, but instead of flowering like the hydrangea in late Summer, it opens lemon yellow typically 'globe' shaped blooms in APRIL and MAY on 18-inch stems. In this way one is able to make full use of all the aspects provided in a well planned border, and use the shadiest areas for plants which enjoy cooler, moister conditions, and the more exposed areas for those which are hardy.

Veronica or Speedwell includes herbaceous perennials which will grow in most soils. Prepare the bed with well rotted compost or moist peat to make certain the roots have plenty of moisture. In a dry soil growth is stunted and there are fewer flowers. No set time can be given as to how frequently the plants will need dividing – in some soils every 3 years, in others they will grow happily for 5. Lift the roots in Spring and replant only the strong, healthy young outer growths.

Veronica gentianoides 'Variegata' has cream and green leaves and blue flowers on 9-inch stems. Veronica 'Crater Lake Blue' is a first class border plant, the bright blue flowers are carried on 15-inch stems.

Vibernum x bodnantense is a most reliable Winter flowering shrub over the widest range of soils and climates. A medium sized bush, about 6 feet high, covered with sweetly scented rose pink flowers on a Winter day is a heart warming sight. It is easily cultivated but a sheltered position is advisable, not so much for the shrubs sake but for the comfort of those who stop to enjoy the flowers. To complement the pink vibernum an underplanting of Snowdrop, *Galanthus nivalis* is effective. The bulbs are easier to move just as the flowers fade, but failing this, should be planted up in AUGUST to SEPTEMBER.

Viola are happiest growing in a place that is shaded during the hottest part of the day. A packet of mixed seed sown in JULY will give seedlings large enough to go out amongst the shrubs in mid-SEPTEMBER. They can be interplanted with the variegated hosta whose impressive foliage makes such an excellent weed-suppressing ground cover. Work peat or well rotted compost into the soil before planting, then mulch each Spring with the same material.

Neat, compact herbaceous plants and shrubs may be used together with bulbs and annuals to fill in the area along the border front.

Points to note

Shrubs or trees should not generally be planted deeper than the mark on the stem which shows the depth to which it was planted in the nursery. Rhododendrons must be planted with the root ball level with the soil surface, then a mulch of peat on the soil to cover the exposed roots to provide the cool, moist, acid conditions this shrubs enjoys. Deep planting can kill rhododendrons. Keep all shrubs well watered, both leaves and roots the first year.

Feed each year in MARCH with a complete fertilizer: nitrogen, phosphates and potash at the rate of 2 oz per sq. yard. A mulch of rotted compost, manure or peat will keep the soil in good physical condition and control weeds. When planting in grass, keep a clear area of at least 30 inches across around the stem of the tree or shrub.

Pruning is necessary to train the trees in the formative years and thereafter to maintain it in good health, also to emphasise the good qualities for which it is grown; flowers, leaves or stem. Each year prune away dead, diseased or crossing wood, then any other branches which detract from the overall characteristic outline of the tree or shrub. When in doubt, do not prune, just leave them alone.

Young shrubs should have dead flower heads removed, especially lilacs, rhododendrons and heathers. A good general rule, if pruning must be done, is shrubs which flower on the previous years growth, forsythia or weigela are examples, may be dealt with immediately the flowers fade. Those which flower on growth made the same year, *Buddleia daviddi* and *Fuchsia magellanica* should be pruned in early MARCH.

Monthly calendar of work

JANUARY

When soil conditions permit, prick over the soil between Spring bedding plants to let in air and moisture. Make certain no plants have been lifted by frost.

Bring bulbs for forcing into the house.

Plant up roses as they arrive from the nursery if weather is favourable.

FEBRUARY

Lift and divide herbaceous plants in the mixed border.

At the end of the month prune clematis and other shrubs which flower on current seasons shoots.

Do any hard pruning on established trees while they are still dormant – paint wood with protective covering.

Sow seed of antirrhinums and similar bedding plants requiring a long growing season, in a heated greenhouse or on a window sill indoors.

Pot up annuals sown in AUGUST for Spring flowering indoors.

Start to prune climbing roses.

MARCH

Take delphiniums cuttings when shoots are being thinned.

Do any repairs to the turf edge along the mixed border – choose a day when the surface is dry enough.

Take cuttings of geraniums, fuchsia, salvia.

Start begonia tubers into growth in moist peat.

Make the main sowing of bedding annuals under glass.

Prick out the annuals from seed sown last month when they are large enough to handle.

Bed out wallflowers, forget-me-nots and polyanthus if this work was not completed in the Autumn.

The foliage house plants can be repotted now, just as they start into growth.

Flowering plants – fuchsia, pelargoniums etc may also be potted on as time permits.

Sow seeds of shrubs and herbaceous perennials in a frame or greenhouse.

Complete the planting up of the roses and deciduous shrubs by the month end.

Prune H.T. and floribunda roses.

APRIL

Plant evergreen shrubs.

Layer rambling roses if new stock is required.

Put air on the house plants during the hottest part of the day.

Continue to prick off seedlings as required.

Start to rest cyclamen, poinsettia and other Winter flowering plants as the leaves yellow.

Take cuttings of Winter flowering begonia.

Prune fuchsia back hard to encourage strong growth.

Sow hardy annuals outdoors to give colour down the mixed border until the shrubs grow in.

Pot up geraniums, begonia, salvia etc when they are large enough.

Apply fertilizer to rose beds which should be cleaned of weeds then mulched with rotted manure or compost.

MAY

Prune forsythia as it finishes flowering.

Transfer bedding plants to frames for hardening off.

Make up hanging baskets so they are established for moving to the patio or terrace in early JUNE.

Plant out viola and pansies.

Sow *Primula obconica* for flowering indoors.

Stake herbaceous perennials, a dressing of fertilizer may be worked in at the same time.

Keep a watch on the roses for pest and diseases – start preventative spraying.

Slugs could be a nuisance, eating young growth on the perennials – put down slug pellets.

JUNE

Clear Spring bedding, heel in the tulips, polyanthus etc in nursery beds.

Feed house plants in full growth.

Prepare beds and plant up the Summer bedding plants.

Pot on Spring struck cuttings of fuchsia and pelargoniums.

Trim hedges as required.

Disbud H.T. roses where exhibition quality flowers are required.

Plant up tubs, window boxes and other containers with Summer bedding.

As the bulbs die down in the shrub border, plant half-hardy annuals to hide them.

Prune shrubs which flowered in MAY – cytisus, *Clematis montana*, etc.

Transfer cyclamen and cineraria from seedtrays to pots.

Thin hardy annual sown direct.

JULY

Solanum, hydrangea etc in frames for flowering indoors will need regular watering and feeding.

Pot cyclamen into flowering pots.

Sow seeds of forget-me-nots etc in nursery bed.

Remove flowers as they fade on roses, then give the bushes a fertilizer dressing.

Continue to spray roses against pests and diseases.

Tulips heeled in to ripen should be lifted and cleaned for storing.

AUGUST

Continue dead heading roses.

Remove spent flowers from Summer bedding.

Plant out delphinium cuttings rooted in Spring.

Prick off or pot on primula, cineraria etc for flowering indoors during Winter.

Cut out the dead flowers on herbaceous plants.

Take cuttings of any shrubs where fresh stock is required.

Pot Winter flowering begonias.

Stand house plants outdoors during rain to freshen up the foliage.

Cyclamen corms rested during the Summer should be started into growth.

Hydrangea in the shrub border will benefit from a soaking with the hose pipe if the weather is dry.

SEPTEMBER

Plant up narcissus in pots for forcing, and in the open garden.

Take cuttings of bedding plants.

Continue to spray roses.

Pot lilies for greenhouse culture.

Hyacinths may be potted and placed in a cool place to root – also tulips.

Prune rambler roses and tie in young growths.

Pot on cyclamen seedlings to prevent them becoming pot-bound.

Plant hyacinths and tulips in tubs and window boxes.

Clean up the borders.

Start planting up evergreen shrubs.

Protect tender plants by moving indoors.

Be careful not to over-water house plants as growth slows down.

Gather fallen leaves.

OCTOBER

Continue to plant up evergreen shrubs so that the roots establish before the soil cools down.

Tubs and window boxes should be cleared of Summer bedding.

Replace with hyacinths and tulips to flower in Spring. Polyanthus, forget-me-nots, viola and other Spring bedding may also be planted up while the weather is still mild.

DO NOT over-water house plants as growth slows down – a warning which cannot be repeated too often.

Protect tender Summer bedding plants.

Gather fallen leaves to compost – leaf mould makes good compost to fill tubs and window boxes.

Dry off begonia tubers used in Summer bedding.

NOVEMBER

Rest begonia, gloxinia etc.

Bring cyclamen indoors as flowering starts.

Take hard wood cuttings.

Complete potting of house and greenhouse plants by the middle of the month.

Weed and prick over the soil down the mixed border.

Clean up fallen leaves and lightly prune the H.T. and floribunda roses. Burn the debris to destroy fungal spores.

Cut back the remaining herbaceous.

Complete all bulb planting this month.

DECEMBER

Clean all pots and boxes.

Pay particular attention to house plants used to decorate the house at Christmas. Rest them in cooler conditions occasionally, and sponge down the foliage.

Prepare against mice damaging Spring flowering bulbs, particularly crocus.